D0536925

Children's
Dream Dictionary

19.⁹⁵

10387-53
2R

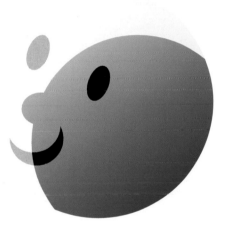

hamlyn

Children's Dream Dictionary

RETIRÉ DE LA COLLECTION UNIVERSELLE
Bibliothèque et Archives nationales du Québec

Amanda Cross

First published in Great Britain in 2002 by
Hamlyn, a division of Octopus Publishing Group Ltd
2–4 Heron Quays, London E14 4JP

Copyright © Octopus Publishing Group Ltd 2002

Distributed in the United States and Canada by Sterling
Publishing Co., Inc. 387 Park Avenue South, New York, NY
10016-8810

All rights reserved. No part of this work may be
reproduced or utilized in any form or by any means,
electronic or mechanical, including photocopying,
recording or by any information storage and retrieval
system, without the prior written permission of the
publisher.

ISBN 0 600 60409 8

A CIP catalogue record for this book is available from the
British Library

Printed and bound in China

10 9 8 7 6 5 4 3 2 1

Contents

Introduction

Where was your child last night? Was he fighting dragons by a huge castle or accompanying his favourite superhero on a trip to the moon? Was she playing with fairies in a green meadow or being chased around the park by a bear wearing a purple dress?

You can guarantee they were somewhere exciting in the realms of their dreams. How well they can recount these nocturnal adventures may be a little erratic, because, like adults, children will wake up sometimes and not be able to remember a thing. At other times they will wake you up in the middle of the night because a scary monster is hiding under their bed.

Usually the most you will hear is a few snippets, a couple of images of weird and wonderful things that may sound like nonsense. But sometimes, if you listen very carefully, you may be able to pick up something that is on your child's mind, as dreams are a pretty good mirror of our inner feelings. Even though young children may not be able to express themselves fully in the verbal sense, this does not mean that they aren't feeling certain things, and when they are asleep then their minds may re-create everything they are secretly wishing for or longing to say.

Conversely, a dream may simply be the work of an over-active imagination. Remember that a child's sense of reality is very different to an adult's understanding of the world. To them, anything is possible: animals can talk, humans can fly, and witches and goblins really do exist.

Whether you want to understand the nature of your child's dreams in order to help banish nightmares or purely to learn more about what makes your child tick, this book is designed to help you view the dream world through the eyes of a child. Have fun.

What are Dreams?

'To sleep, to sleep, perchance to dream'
Hamlet William Shakespeare

Dreams have been the subject of much debate and study since the beginning of time. The ancients thought they were messages from the gods; today we study them from scientific, psychological and physiological standpoints. Some people dismiss dreams as irrelevant, while others use the richness of these nocturnal fantasies to unravel the complexities of their lives, unearth deep-seated problems and even to arrive at important decisions.

Whatever your attitude towards dreaming, we all do it. Even babies are believed to dream in the womb, and all children dream as part of a process through which they make sense of the world around them. So, could it be that dreaming is essential to our well-being – is the need for dreaming one of the major reasons that we go to sleep?

One thing is certain: we all need to sleep. This phenomenon is not restricted to humans. Mammals, birds, fish and reptiles all sleep, and some plants close up their petals as the sun sets, re-opening them just before it rises again. Our sleep patterns are also linked to the rising and setting of the sun, with our 'internal clock' giving us precise signals as to when to sleep and when to re-awake. These cycles are known as circadian rhythms.

Why we sleep

As adults, we spend about 30 per cent of our lives sleeping, children about 50 per cent. So what is the purpose of sleep? We all know that after a few nights of interrupted sleep, even the most energetic and cheerful of adults and children will become grumpy and will not function as well as usual. Concentration and *joie de vivre* are replaced by lethargy and bad temper.

It was once thought that we needed to sleep to rest our bodies, and there is evidence that links sleep with a time for physical repair and restoration. Our metabolism slows down and our immune system concentrates on fighting any infection or other damage. But studies have also shown that when people sleep, their bodies are continually shifting position, sometimes turning over up to 20 times in one night. We all know that when we check on our children in bed at night,

they have usually managed to end up in a totally different position to that in which we left them earlier.

REM and NREM

So do we sleep to rest our weary brains? Do we shut off totally at night? Are we dead to the world? It would appear not. In the 1950s, a group of scientists in Chicago identified the two stages of sleep known as REM (Rapid Eye Movement) and NREM (Non Rapid Eye Movement). When we first go to sleep, we fall into a phase of quiet NREM sleep. This lasts up to 90 minutes, followed by a period of REM sleep that lasts about 10 minutes. As we alternate between these two types of sleep, the NREM stages become shorter and the REM stages longer.

During REM sleep, our faces twitch and our eyes move rapidly under our eyelids. This is when we are believed to dream most vividly. During scientific studies, sleepers who were woken during periods of REM sleep could describe dreams in detail, whereas those woken in an NREM phase were less likely to be able to remember their dreams, even if they thought they had been dreaming.

Different types of dreams

Creative dreams

Many artists and writers have been inspired by images that have appeared in their dreams. Some of the most famous paintings and works literature have been produced because of dream-time inspiration. Robert Louis Stevenson was inspired to write both *The Strange Case of Dr Jekyll and Mr Hyde* and *Treasure Island* as the result of dreams, and Mary Shelley conjured up the disturbing tale of Frankenstein's monster while sleeping.

Many of the works of William Shakespeare, including *The Tempest*, *Hamlet*, *Macbeth* and *A Midsummer Night's Dream*, have very strong dream themes, to the extent that understanding their meaning is totally reliant on recognizing the association between dreams and waking life. Could it be that Shakespeare actually dreamt up these plays?

Lucid

In lucid dreams, the dreamer is aware that he is dreaming and can actually control the action: it is a bit like directing your own personal film. This takes a degree of practice and skill – some lucid dreamers even claim to meet up with each other in their dreams, and wake to discover that they have both been dreaming about the same things.

The most beneficial effect of lucid dreaming is that when a person is having a bad dream, he can either wake himself up, or decide what he wants to happen in the dream and manipulate the outcome. This is something that can help children who suffer from nightmares.

Nightmares

Nightmares are usually the manifestation of personal fears and mean that something in the dreamer's life needs to be confronted. The most common themes for nightmares are experiencing a violent attack or seeing a friend experience one; trying to get away from something or someone; trying and failing to get somewhere on time; and suffocating or paralysis.

Sometimes these nightmares will be related directly to the source of the fear or anxiety that causes them, or they may just occur when a person is stressed – at exam time, for example.

Prophetic

With these dreams, the dreamer claims to be able to see into the future and predict events. This can be a form of warning for either the dreamer or somebody close to him, and there are many examples of these types of dream coming true in real life.

Recurring

If a person has the same dream over and over again, then something in the waking world is troubling him and needs to be sorted out. The subject matter and time of the dream should be analysed. Does it occur concurrently with certain factors in the dreamer's real world? Could it be linked to stress, or important events or people in the dreamer's life?

Visions

As with prophetic dreams, these can predict a future event, but in this instance may occur when the person is awake. One of the most famous examples of a visionary was Joan of Arc, who believed herself to be the saviour of France as a result of listening to the voices that came to her in her dreams, voices that she insisted came from God. Unfortunately for Joan, the English church decided that she was actually communicating with Satan, and burned her at the stake.

What can we learn from dreams?

So why do we dream? What can we learn from the experiences that our minds create when we are deep in sleep? Science has provided us with answers to many of the questions concerning when we dream and the physical changes that take place while we are asleep – but as for why we dream, that is a different matter entirely.

Theories abound as to the point of dreams. Some say that the hindbrain – the area of the brain that transmits messages – winds down when we sleep, but the cortex – the part of the brain that interprets these signals – needs a certain amount of stimulus to keep it ticking over. In response, the hindbrain gives out the occasional signal, but this has little or no foundation in reality to keep it going.

Others believe that the cortex is dumping random information for which we have no further use, and that this is the reason why so many people cannot remember their dreams in the morning. We dream in order to sift out the knowledge and events we no longer require, leaving more room for the important information we need to retain –

in other words, dreaming is a nightly mental clean-up.

But the theory that seems to explain why dreams have always been viewed as an important part of the human psyche is that the cortex will continue to interpret the outside world as we sleep, and will try to make sense of the chaotic messages the brain has sent it. So, issues that we have buried and neglected to deal with are free to be addressed by the subconscious mind.

Of course, no matter how deeply a person has drifted into sleep, the brain will still be susceptible to certain external influences. Often a thunderstorm, an alarm clock or even the physical need to pass water will appear in the dream. It is important to isolate such factors when attempting to unravel the possible meanings of dreams.

Children's dreams

Children's dreams may be different from those of an adult, in that they are not as sophisticated and complex, but the reasons why children dream are nevertheless the same. Counsellor Brenda Mallon discusses these in her book *Children Dreaming* (Penguin, 1989), and puts forward five possible explanations for children's dreams:

Dreams can help a child to sort out the events of the day. Children's dreams are an echo of daily occurrences that need to be assimilated and understood.

Dreams act as a vehicle for wish-fulfilment. This enables children to live out their greatest fantasies and may allow a degree of escapism from unhappiness or boredom.

Dreams help a child to prepare for a future event. A child may anticipate and act out a scenario to which he is looking forward to or is nervous about, such as a holiday or starting at a new school.

Dreams help a child to sort out problems. By allowing reflection on an issue, a child may be able to work out a possible resolution, even though this will be on a fairly basic level.

Dreams help a child to communicate. Dreams act as the bridge to the unconscious conflicts, anxieties and fears that a child may be experiencing.

How to interpret dreams

Dream interpreters

People have been trying to make sense of dreams for centuries – Artemidorus, Freud and Jung being a few of the better known ones. Many books have been written detailing the symbolism of the various elements that occur in dreams.

Of course, the world today is a very different place to the one that the earlier interpreters inhabited. Artemidorus lived in Asia in the second century AD, Freud first published his theories in Vienna, Austria, in 1899, and Jung was writing down his thoughts on the matter in Switzerland around 1916. As visionary, ground-breaking and influential as these men were, they lived in a different environment to the one we face in the twenty-first century. The work of Freud and Jung may have provided the basis for most of the dream books that have been written since, but they were nevertheless born in an era that had not yet seen space travel, computer technology, television and videos, high divorce rates, the tabloid press and much, much more. These factors all have to be added to the equation when evaluating the dreams of today's children.

Dream influences

The sheer weight of the visual and mental stimuli that even the youngest child experiences nowadays is enormous. Of course, there have always been plenty of things for children to have nightmares about – wars, murders and mythical monsters are all relatively commonplace, whatever the century or culture into which a child is born. Most fairy tales feature 'good-against-evil' plot lines, as well as highlighting skulduggery and violence. Even many nursery rhymes have somewhat sinister overtones.

Dream images

Some aspects of dreams will always be universally common: for example, the sensation of falling or flying occurs regularly, no matter what the cultural or social background of the dreamer. However, there are many other elements, such as characters or places, which will take on a very personal symbolism for each individual, depending on their experience and understanding of life.

Obviously, a child's experience is very limited. This is particularly true of the pre-school youngster, whose life revolves around the family and home. Children are still trying to make sense of the world around them, and their sense of reality is different to that of an adult. While an adult has absorbed large amounts of information, gone through many different experiences, and developed subconscious and conscious associations between objects, characters, events, colours, places, and tastes, a child has a far more simple viewpoint. Children also blend reality with fantasy, which can make deciphering their dreams more difficult.

So, when faced with your offspring's disjointed and sometimes surreal accounts of his nocturnal adventures, how do you begin to make sense of the information he is giving you?

The four rules

To begin with, you should obviously take into account your child's personality and the circumstances affecting his life at the time of the dream. Think school, think friends and, most definitely, think family.

Then, to make your task a little more straightforward, there are four basic concepts you should consider when attempting to unravel the complexities of your child's dreams.

1 Everything is me

The first principle to grasp is that everything that appears in a child's dream can reflect an aspect of the dreamer. So, you must always consider what is represented by characters, colours, numbers, objects, animals, locations, actions, elements, nature, symbols and occasions.

Mind *thoughts and feelings*

The atmosphere of a dream can shed light on how a child is feeling about things in his daily life. Ask your child to describe the place he visited in his dream. Was it dark and cold, or sunny and bright? Is he describing a place that he knows? Did he feel very scared, or happy to be there? The answers will quite often reflect your child's current emotional state.

Body *health and well-being*

In dreams, solid objects such as buildings and cars reflect the physical body. If your child dreams about a house that is ramshackle or falling down, or a toy that is broken, this could mean he is sick or coming down with an illness. It is quite common for dreams to echo a physical condition: a child may dream of a raging fire if he has a temperature, or about dripping taps and waterfalls when he actually needs to pass water. If you keep a record of dreams, you may be able to spot certain dream-time signals that indicate your child was not fully healthy at the time.

Spirit *personality*

Children come into this world as free spirits which have yet to encounter the various restrictions that parents, schools and society in general will soon impose on them.

They are naturally creative: just give a child a pile of sand, an old box or a lump of clay, and his immediate inclination is to turn it into something else. We all need to express ourselves, and creativity on any level is the ultimate form of expression.

As adults, we find the experience of not being able to be ourselves a frustrating one; a child will feel this too, but will almost certainly not be able to express it verbally. Watch out for images of restriction and confinement in your child's dreams, as these could indicate that his true nature is being held back. It may be time to get out

the paints or turn up the music, and let him express his true character.

2 Cause and effect

All the symbols in dreams are linked to show cause and effect. Sometimes clues are held in the most (apparently) unrelated things. You need to find the symbol that represents the root of the dreamer's problem.

For example, if a child dreams that he is walking willingly into a dungeon, it could indicate that he is a prisoner of his own feelings, and is unable to communicate what it is that is troubling him. If there is a pile of dynamite in the corner of the dungeon, then the child is waiting to explode – that is the effect.

By recognizing problems within in a dream and identifying the current or potential effect, you can help your child deal with the situation before it develops into a behavioural trait that could affect him for the rest of his life.

3 Avoidance tactics

Pay attention to the things in a dream that your child is trying to avoid. This could be a fear, an emotion or a situation, but, either way, it needs to be confronted in daily life. Our dreams urge us to deal with the parts of ourselves we would rather not face. They will not allow us to separate ourselves from issues we try to block out, and with good reason – it is best to

confront those negative elements of our personality as soon as possible. Identify them, then deal with them in order to heal them.

For instance, it is very common for children to dream that they have been left alone or even abandoned by their parents, particularly today when so many marriages end in divorce. It is understandable that a child may listen to parents arguing, hear stories from other children at school, or even have to experience the pain of his mother and father deciding to separate, and will then project this into a deep, dark fear that haunts his dreams. Children are often the first to pick up on domestic turmoil and they will try to blot out the experience during everyday life, but their subconscious invariably gets the better of them. It may be that all a child needs at this stage is reassurance and positive attention from both parents to prove that his fears are unfounded. At the very least, he needs the situation explained to him.

4 I am in control

One very important aspect of dreams is that the dreamer is always responsible for what happened, is happening, can happen and will happen. This rule does not vary.

Things often appear to run out of control in a dream – there are accidents, things get lost, and so on – which inhibit the dreamer's progress. What this usually indicates is that there are character traits within the dreamer that are holding him back, such as reluctance, nervousness or lack of confidence.

If, for example, your child is auditioning for a part in a play, and dreams that the family car breaks down on the way to school the next morning, this could mean that he is feeling less than confident and is scared of failure. Once alerted to this, you, as a parent, can do as much as you can to alleviate those feelings by offering him reassurance.

These four very general rules hold the key to unravelling some dreams and are good basic guidelines, but following them too rigidly and not taking into consideration your child's character and outlook on life will stop you fully interpreting his dreams. Keep your perspective broad and always consider such influences as recent events, current films and literature. The dark, scary house could be the home of your child's most feared cartoon baddie; the broken toy may not mean that he is ailing – he could simply have broken a real one the day before. As for the dungeon and dynamite, could your child's class at school have been studying the story of Guy Fawkes' attempt to blow up the Houses of Parliament?

Identifying each element of your child's dream is often tricky, but you are the person that knows him best, and a combination of the approaches outlined in this book and your natural instinct should help you to find the answers.

Dreams and how they relate to daytime fears

Quite often, the things we are afraid of during the daytime will turn up again in our nightmares. This is particularly true of a very young child, who will tend to experience very literal dreams with little symbolism involved. The object of fear could be something physical, like spiders or dogs, or it could be an image that he has seen on television, such as the villain in a series, or perhaps a danger-ridden cave that featured in a book he has been reading. All this will, of course, be interspersed with heavy amounts of his own fantasy.

Once a child is old enough to go to school, then expect him to have a few more nightmares, simply because he has a lot more to worry about. Imagine the anxiety that even the most confident child feels at the prospect of being thrown into a new environment where, maybe for the first time, he is without a parent or familiar carer.

In this situation, your child is confronted by a large amount of information in a very short time. There are unfamiliar faces to remember, different rules to learn and, of course, the potentially traumatic experience of making friends. It is hardly surprising that he experiences fitful sleep and fear-ridden dreams.

In her book *Your Child's Dreams* (Ballantine Books, 1984), dream specialist Patricia Garfield revealed that the peak time for children's nightmares is between the ages of five and seven. It is surely no coincidence that this is the time at which they are under stress about starting school. As your child gets used to a different environment, the nightmares should abate, but if they continue then you should talk to the teacher and try to get to the root of his anxiety.

Stressful dreams usually represent some daytime problem. If your child dreams regularly about a monster that attacks him, you may be able to convince him that the monster in the dream isn't real. But if by day he is being bullied by a child twice his size, the monster might stay. In this case, the problem should also be solved by day. Similar night-time unrest might occur when your child is changing schools, although obviously the source of bad dreams isn't restricted to school alone.

If there have been a lot of changes or negative experiences in your child's life, these will usually be echoed in the types of dreams he has. Maybe you have recently moved house, or are in the middle of a divorce. It could be simply that you've had to tell your child off recently and this frightened him. If this is the case, then you may be that monster who keeps chasing him.

In addition, a child's circumstances will alter the fabric of his dreams immensely. If he lives in an urban environment, for example, the source of his fears will be different to that of a child who lives in a more rural setting.

As children get older, the fantasy figures will subside and their dreams will become related more closely to events in the real world, so be prepared for dreams which reveal that your child is feeling unprotected and unsafe. It is very rare today that television news bulletins are without some terrible story, and it is amazing how much your child will pick up and worry about.

Remember, too, that dreams may be the only way children can express how they are really feeling, and if a dream is disturbing your child, then you cannot simply ignore it.

Coping with nightmares and night terrors

Night terrors can occur when the brain switches between REM and NREM sleep, and becomes divided between being asleep and being awake. During this phase a child may sit up, talk, scream or even wander around – 'sleep walking'. She will awake confused and agitated, scream in terror at an invisible threat and be unresponsive to attempts to calm her. This state can last for up to 20 minutes. There will be no specific images that cause the fear, as there are with nightmares, and next morning your child will have no recollection of what happened.

The best thing you can do is to protect her from harm, restricting access to stairs or furniture, and gently coax her back into bed. Leave the light on low and stay until she has calmed down and dropped back to sleep.

The brain-switching mechanism develops between infancy and the age of ten, so most episodes occur within this age group. As long as they take place no more than three times per year, there is no need to seek help.

If bedtime is a struggle

First work out why your child says 'But I'm not tired!' Some children may need more attention; others are simply asserting their independence. Young children could also be experiencing some separation anxiety. Many children are scared of being alone in a dark room, as it is easy for them to imagine monsters under the bed. For others, bedtime brings with it the possibility of yet another nightmare.

It is usually at around the age of three that nightmares begin to feature in a child's life. Suddenly the world appears bigger and more frightening, and she may also now be exposed to some scary fantasy figures in children's television programmes, which further fuel her active imagination.

One factor that could have a profound effect is a child's understanding of death. She may be confused as to the difference between death and sleep – never describe death as 'going to sleep' as she may believe that she won't ever wake up.

Before bed

Monitor the television. Be very careful about what you let your child watch before bed. Frightening programmes will intensify her underlying fears.

Tackle fears. Talk to your child about her fears and explain that she is safe and you won't let anything happen to her. Leave the bedroom door open a crack and the hall light on. Never offer to stay until she falls asleep, as she could become dependent on your presence every night.

Set routines. Give your child at least half an hour to relax and get ready for bed. Comforting rituals include taking a bath and reading non-scary bedtime stories. Predictability will increase your child's sense of security.

Establish a consistent bedtime. Once you have chosen a bedtime that will give your child enough sleep (typically 11–12 hours for a three- to five-year-old, 8–10 hours for older children), be sure to enforce it. All children benefit from a regular sleep schedule.

If your child wakes from a nightmare

• First reassure her with a big hug.
• Explain that the bad dream was a story she made up in her own head.
• Do not force her to talk about the nightmare, unless she wants to, as this may upset her again.
• Turn on the light for a while so that she realizes that everything is as it was before she went to bed.
• Talk about something cheerful and try to take her mind off the dream.
• Stay with her until she starts to fall back to sleep, then tell her where you will be, before leaving.
• If all else fails, take your child into bed with you.

Next morning

• This is a better time to talk to your child about the nightmare. Do not be surprised if she remembers very little. Again, do not force her to talk if she doesn't want to.
• Re-emphasize that the dream isn't real, and listen carefully to what your child says – many nightmares are a direct result of the previous day's activities.
• Look for indications of pressure or anxiety: was the dream based on anything or anybody in your child's life? Does it have a running theme, such as being chased or being late?
• If you can make sense of the dream, explain it as simply as possible to your child and then leave it. Making a big issue of it will over-dramatize it in her mind.
• If the dream is recurring, you need to discover and deal with the real problem, otherwise the nightmares are likely to continue. This may involve talking to your child's teacher or carer, siblings and even friends, to find out if there is anything troubling her that she is not able or willing to tell you.

Friendly nightmare figures

There are some other tactics you can try to help your child get a restful night's sleep.

The Baku

In Japan, people used to carry with them (and some still do) a small sculpture in the form of a mystical animal called a Baku, which means 'dream eater'. It is believed that if the person who owns it, rubs over it a couple a times before he goes to sleep, he is then blessed with beautiful dreams. But if he does have a nightmare, he must call the animal's name and the creature will eat the nightmare immediately.

Maybe you could get your child the equivalent of a modern Baku. Traditionally they are alarming-looking creatures, so, instead, you could nominate a favourite teddy bear or other cuddly toy and invest it with such nightmare-eating powers. It's the principle that counts.

Protective clothing

Why not try sending your child to bed in 'power sleeping wear'? By this I mean a shirt or pyjamas emblazoned with an image of his favourite superhero, or something powerful like a dragon – whatever your child may associate with feeling safe and protected. This should help him banish his fear.

Using positive examples

Another important thing to do – particularly if your child is frightened of creatures like wolves or lions, or the more imaginary objects of fear such as aliens, ghosts or monsters – is to find books or films that cast these things in a positive light. So, if your child has dreams about a monster, read books about children who become friends with monsters; if your child has nightmares about falling, read books or show films about flying. Obviously, you must be careful to avoid anything that portrays these things as terrifying or threatening.

As a child gets older, he will understand that lions, tigers and other wild animals are either safely housed in a zoo or live in game parks, well away from his bedroom door. He will also be able to understand that many of the nightly spooks and monsters that plagued him in his earlier years were simply figments of his active imagination.

But for a small child, the things that go bump in the night are very, very real.

Tips from the Senoi

One society that seemed to get the whole dream thing right was the Senoi, a tribe that lived in the mountains of Malaysia and had a society free of crime and mental illness.

Dreams were very important in the life of the Senoi. Every morning, the entire family discussed what had happened in their dreams the night before. This had a profound effect on their children: by the time a Senoi child reached his teens, nightmares were non-existent and all his dreams were positive experiences.

The reason the Senoi did not suffer from neurosis or psychoses was due to the way they taught their children to handle their dreams.

The most important rule was to confront and conquer any danger in the dream. For instance, if a child dreamed that a tiger had attacked him, his parents would tell him that such dream-tigers could not hurt him and would encourage the child to attack the tiger the next time. If the child felt he wasn't strong enough, he could call a 'dream-friend' – usually a Senoi elder – to help him. If the danger was fire, the child should put it out with water; if he dreamed of falling from a mountain, he would be able to land softly or to fly.

The child's dreams were seen as voyages of discovery with unlimited possibilities. He was encouraged to have as much pleasure as possible in the dream, and always exit from it on a positive experience. Such was the power of this belief that even if the dreamer died in the dream, he would imagine himself to be reborn in a better and much stronger body.

It was also important to make as many friends as possible in the dream. Hostile characters could also be 'conquered' by becoming the child's friend – a logical move if you consider that every element of the dream represents a facet of the dreamer. If the character remained aggressive, the child was advised to attack him, either on his own or with a dream friend. The defeated character would have to make friends with the child and pass on a dream gift as a token of goodwill.

These dream gifts were a very important part of the dream. The Senoi spent a lot of time creating items that they had seen in their dreams. These might be a painting, a woodcarving or perhaps a piece of music. So, not only were the dreams of the Senoi lucid, they were also creative.

Regrettably, the idyllic society of the Senoi was almost entirely destroyed during World War II, following its decimation by the Japanese occupation of Malaysia. But the tribe's principles were adopted by many dream interpreters, including Jung, and provided a template that, if fully explored, could lead to far greater understanding of our dream worlds and the subconscious messages held within them.

Keeping a dream diary

One way of integrating the principles of the Senoi into your child's life is to show her how to keep a dream diary. This is a very simple way of recording dreams and encouraging your child to have less fear of her night-time adventures.

All you need is a big pad of paper in which she can write or draw what she experienced the night before. If your child cannot translate all the details onto the paper in either words or pictures, you can write down some of this information for her. By keeping the diary you will have a record of her reactions to certain events, and it will allow you to build up a comprehensive picture of the inner workings of your child's mind. You never know – you may even discover that she has prophetic powers!

Keeping a diary also allows for a

Make sure to include the following:

- Date
- The atmosphere and how your child was feeling
- The location and theme of the dream
- Characters, objects, symbols and signs
- Your child's own actions
- Colours and conversations

further stage, which dream expert Patricia Garfield calls 're-dreaming'. This is very useful if your child has been suffering from bad dreams. Once she has written down or drawn the dream in the diary, ask her to close her eyes and imagine how she would have liked the dream to have been. Would she have wanted to attack or make friends with the monster? Fly above the scene? Find buried treasure? Then get your child to write another version or draw another picture of her new dream. This will reinforce in her mind the fact that she has power over what goes on in her dreams at night, and may lead to her being able actively to control and participate in her dreams – ideally, so that the nightmare element is totally eradicated.

It is also important to remember that many dreams are happy dreams that give your youngster the opportunity to explore her fantasies. Whatever the nature of her night-time escapades, by unravelling the workings of her inner self you provide yourself with greater knowledge, which in turn will enable you to help her develop into a well-adjusted child with a high level of self-understanding and the ability to express her feelings and emotions.

Dream interpretation
Animals

Animals

Symbolically, animals in dreams can reflect our most basic instincts, such as caring or aggression, and echo our own characteristics.

Children are surrounded by animals almost from the moment they are born. Walk into any child's bedroom and you will normally see a whole host of cuddly soft toys in the shape of animals of all kinds.

In children's literature and cartoons, animals can fly, talk, be heroes or villains or be a best friend. A child's understanding of an animal's characteristics is largely formed by what he watches or reads, and it is this understanding of each animal that will give you clues to aspects of your child's own character and how he may be feeling.

Feathers and fur

Birds

Birds are generally positive symbols in a dream. As adults, we understand the concept of a dove being a bird of peace, or an eagle representing our higher self, but a child is more likely to experience a bird as simply big or small, friendly or scary – and it could come in any colour under the sun.

If your child dreams about large birds with sharp beaks and massive wings which keep swooping down at them, this could indicate that something is making her nervous. Could she have seen something on television or a film that may have given her this fear? Has she been anywhere where birds behave like this? Is there anything in your child's life that is making her feel threatened?

If the birds are flying off into the distance, this may signify disappointment. Has a special treat been cancelled at the last moment? It can also mean that your child feels something is flying away from her. Have you recently pointed out that she has been squandering her pocket money? Maybe it is time to buy your child a money box.

Has your child described watching, or

imagining herself to be, a bird flying way up in the sky? This could be an early sign of high aspirations: perhaps you are looking at a future political leader or a famous actor. Your child may be destined for great things.

Domestic cats

If a child likes them, **cats** can reflect a positive, feminine side of her nature. If not, then they can represent spiteful behaviour.

Seen traditionally as a sign of good (or, in some cultures, bad) luck, If they happen to be black and cross your path, cats are often a child's first contact with a live animal. Instinctively, she will want to hold and pet it, but all too often the cat will run away, or even turn around and scratch if your well-meaning offspring's attentions are too rough or ill-timed. From the child's perspective, this can be very frustrating and disappointing, as she simply wants to be affectionate and friendly. Even though she may not wholly understand the concept, this fickle behaviour is something your child will certainly have to contend with at some point in her life, particularly when she starts school and begins to make friends.

If your child dreams of cats that turn their backs, run away or scratch, then this may really be happening in the playground. Has she fallen out with a best friend? Or could she be feeling that someone very close and trusted has let her down?

Conversely, if your child dreams of playful kittens this is a good sign, for it means she is happy and contented.

But beware if the cat is sneaking about in the dream, as this could mean that your child has a guilty conscience about something.

Dogs

Dogs

It is easy to understand why a small child could be frightened of **dogs**, particularly if he generally has little or no contact with them. Even though they are usually portrayed as 'man's best friend', a barking dog, no matter what size, must seem scary to a young child. The message is loud and clear: don't come any nearer.

If your child has ever had a negative encounter with a dog, then potentially this could be the stuff of nightmares. However, as he gets older he will learn that barking can also mean that the dog needs attention; he will also begin to appreciate that dogs can be loyal, protective friends.

When dogs appear in a child's dreams, they can symbolize a warning, be drawing their attention to something, or be indicative of his relationship with his friends. For example, if the dog turns and growls at your child it may mean that someone has said something horrible or done something nasty to him.

A dog that keeps trying to bite your child means that the dog is trying to draw his attention to something. What else appears in the dream?

If the dog keeps barking, this is a reminder that your child has to finish something – is that school project completed yet?

If the dog is friendly, then the dream is about a good friend. An unfriendly dog means that a friend is being disloyal.

Foxes

A big red dog with a huge bushy tail can only be a **fox**. These creatures are invariably characterized as sly, wily and

fast moving. They represent a cunning trickster, waiting until the cover of darkness before getting up to no good. Is there someone in your child's life that he either dislikes or of whom he is particularly wary? Or could it be that your child is especially suspicious by nature?

Wolves

Is it possible that your child was not actually describing a dog? It could have been a **wolf**, particularly if you have just finished reading the story of Little Red Riding Hood. Wolves are supposed to signify hard times ahead and in general are a bad omen. We have all heard the expression 'a wolf in sheep's clothing' – for Little Red Riding Hood it was her granny's clothes, but the implication is the same: beware of people who present themselves as something they are not.

Rodents and bats

Rabbits

Rabbits traditionally represent fertility and faithfulness in love, with a white rabbit symbolizing our inner world.

Remember the rabbit in *Alice in Wonderland*, who went scurrying around all over the place, fretting that he was late? If he represented a part of Alice, the dreamer, this would reveal that she was anxious about something. Could this be the case with your child? Or was she simply dreaming about a favourite pet or cuddly toy? What was the rabbit doing? This could reveal how your child is feeling at a deeper level.

Rabbits and **hares** are also symbolic of self-sacrifice, so is there anything that your child needs to let go of before moving on?

If you are starting a new business venture and your child repeatedly dreams of rabbits, this is a good omen as it means you will do very well.

Rats

Rats appearing in dreams can mean that the dreamer is experiencing many small, irritating problems, but essentially can be objects of real fear, particularly if your child has had negative experiences of them.

It is very common to call someone a 'rat' if he has behaved badly, and very rarely are they seen as positive characters. In children's literature, they are usually portrayed as sneaky and untrustworthy, so if they appear in dreams they could be representing somebody in your child's life who also displays those characteristics. Has your child come home from school complaining about any of her classmates? Or could it be that your youngster feels she has been a bit of a rat herself, maybe telling tales about her best friend?

Mice

Even though cartoon **mice** such as Mickey and Minnie Mouse, Jerry and, more recently, Stuart Little have larger-than-life personalities, this is not how mice are generally perceived.

Unless your child has access to mice at school or pet mice at home, probably the only time she will see a mouse is running across a floor causing havoc, or being dropped from a cat's mouth.

Mice are timid creatures that lie low until danger has passed. Is the mouse of your child's dreams a reflection of a shy nature? Does your child have problems joining in with other kids' games? Or could it be that someone is nibbling away at her self-confidence? Is there a superstar sibling around, who succeeds at everything and may be putting a brother or sister in the shade?

Bats

The Chinese associate **bats** with good fortune, wealth, health and a long life, but in general bats are seen as symbols of the forces of darkness because they only come out when the sun has gone down. Even the Caped Crusader, Batman himself, is only ever seen with his mask on, a mysterious figure whose true identity is known only to Robin and his faithful butler.

So what could be lurking in the darkness? What is it that your child secretly fears or does not fully understand? Could she feel that someone around her is wearing a mask, perhaps being nice to her in the presence of others and then revealing their true nature when they are on their own? Maybe an older sibling is hitting out at your child when you turn your back, but behaving like an angel in front of you.

Wild animals

Lions and tigers

Lions and tigers represent courage, nobility and pride. They conjure up both fear and admiration in adults and children alike. Is a big cat chasing your child in his dreams? If so, it could be that the lion or tiger represents either the courageous and brave part of the child, or a person with whom he associates those qualities. Is he subconsciously telling himself to be braver about a certain situation? What is he fearful of?

Has your child shown signs of being reluctant to go to school? Has he been the victim of bullying? Have you noticed anything unusual lately, such as your child's pocket money disappearing too quickly? These are tell-tale signs that you should look for, along with slightly withdrawn behaviour.

Is your child due to start a new school? This can be a concern and can be the cause of a few nightmares.

This is the sort of dream you should try to get to the bottom of, as it indicates real anxiety. Lions, tigers and all the other big cats represent feminine qualities, so could there be a female teacher who has been telling off your child, or have there been mother-and-child issues lately? Maybe your child is not listening to this woman's advice, even though deep down he knows he should.

You could suggest to him that the lion or tiger is there to help him overcome his difficulties, and if he dreams about it again, he should make friends with it and ask it what to do.

Elephants

Elephants are seen as big, reliable friends and are associated with a long memory, endurance and power. They are rarely portrayed in a negative light in children's literature, so despite their immense size, they are usually not an object of fear to a child.

Elephants occur in very positive dreams and can represent an older trusted male, such as an uncle, teacher or possibly godfather. They may also be an indication of an environmentally-aware child who has been taught or read about endangered species and is perhaps expressing concern within the dream.

These mammals can also indicate that the dreamer is determined to succeed despite facing massive obstacles. You can rest assured that your child will never give up trying, even though sometimes the tasks may seem too much and his progress ponderously slow.

Bears

Bears can represent very different things to children, depending on where in the world they are living. To a child in North America, bears spell danger; to an Australian child, a bear is probably a cuddly koala, the national emblem; to a western European child, the nearest she ever gets to a bear is her teddy. All have very different connotations and implications within a dream.

In general, bears are viewed as protective, powerful creatures that can overcome most things, as in nature they have no natural predator or enemy – except humans.

They are also a symbol of brute force and can often appear in dreams as a sign that there is an overbearing father, or father figure (such as a stepfather, teacher or older relative) in your child's life.

Conversely, if your child dreams that a bear is hugging her to the point of breathlessness, this is more likely to be a suggestion that a mother, or mother figure, is being too domineering.

Ask your child to describe the bear, and establish whether it is a real bear or a toy. Obviously, a dream in which your child flies to Mars with her favourite teddy is far less worrying than if she were to describe hiding from a big black bear that wanted to bite her.

Monkeys

Monkeys are stereotypically mischievous and playful, but are also not to be trusted. Remember King Louis in *The Jungle Book*? He pretended to be Mowgli's friend, but all he wanted was the secret of man's great fire and then he would happily have given Mowgli to the man-eating tiger, Sheerkhan.

Dreaming of monkeys could mean that your child has friends who are kind to her face, but not behind her back. They are taking advantage in order to get what they want. Your child probably realizes this on a subconscious level, but does not want to believe it. Does she have the sort of friends who only come round to borrow her bike and play with her toys, but never return the favour? Are they reckless with your child's belongings and always leave things broken or ruined? Maybe it is time to encourage your child to broaden or even change her circle of friends.

Monkeys can also represent the childish, immature side of ourselves, and by dreaming of them we are recognizing that sometimes this side of us can be irritating to other people. Has your child had a ticking-off lately for being annoying?

Reptiles and amphibians

Alligators and crocodiles

Alligators and crocodiles represent a deep primordial fear within human beings. They signify danger, and signal caution. If life is a flowing river, then these creatures are the hidden dangers lurking just beneath the surface – the biggest worry being that sometimes you don't even realize they are there until it is too late. What you see is a harmless log floating in the middle of the river; then, when you get close, suddenly SNAP! In the tale of Peter Pan, even Captain Hook is scared of the crocodile that had once bitten off his hand and was intent on finishing the job.

Big, snappy alligators and crocodiles in your child's dreams are a warning of underhand behaviour; even if they are doing nothing much but lazing around, these creatures are nevertheless an indication of adverse influences, and a sure sign that your little one is feeling frightened or apprehensive about something. Is he starting a new school or playgroup? This is certainly an occasion for some extra comfort and reassurance.

An alligator in your child's dreams may suggest that he is being thick-skinned or insensitive towards someone else – not a particularly unusual occurrence with young children – so remember this when observing your child's behaviour towards his friends and family.

Toads and frogs

Toads and frogs symbolize major change or transformation, developing as they do from spawn, to swimming tadpoles, to completely different creatures with arms, legs and lungs that breathe air. To a child they are probably ugly, but certainly not frightening. In fact, many children will happily play with these amphibians – if they can manage to catch one.

Is there something your child may want to change about his personality or image? Does he hate his glasses or braces? Does he want to wear his fashionable clothes to school instead of school uniform? Alternatively, is he aware that he is not being quite as good as he could be? Maybe his bedroom is not being tidied up as regularly as you ask, or has he been giving the childminder a difficult time the minute you turn your back?

It sounds as if your child needs to make changes in his life or behaviour, so your best approach is to play up the positive, then deal with the negative. Remember: it only takes a kiss to turn a frog into a handsome prince.

Frogs are also related to medical problems, so keep a lookout for any symptoms of ill health.

Slithering creatures

Snakes

Snakes are the manifestation of human energy and are revered in many cultures. They are also associated with fertility and healing. Nevertheless, we still use phrases like 'a snake in the grass' or 'a viper in the bosom' to describe someone who is treacherous and ready to strike when you least expect it.

Fictional characters such as Ka, the snake in *The Jungle Book*, reinforce this image in the minds of children and they see snakes as creatures who are not to be trusted.

If your child is dreaming about snakes, something is afoot and someone is around she instinctively does not trust.

Lizards and chameleons

Lizards and chameleons represent something that is ugly on the outside but are not necessarily horrible, and, like toads and frogs, they are symbols of personal transformation. In temperate climates they aren't as common as frogs and toads, so your child may only have seen one in a zoo, or perhaps scurrying over a sun-baked wall while you were on holiday in hotter climes. Maybe your youngster has been studying them at school. On the other hand, you may live in a warmer area that is frequented by lizards. But however your child may have become aware of these reptiles, what are they doing in her dreams?

According to ancient shamanic beliefs, lizards and chameleons could be the carriers of important spiritual messages. Did your child have a conversation with the creature in her dream? If so, what did it say?

Lizards and chameleons are a positive omen. If, however, your child was scared, make sure that she wasn't trying to describe a dinosaur. It is easy to see how a child could get the two confused.

Worms

Wriggling **worms** hold great attraction for many young children; they have a positive desire to get their hands in the mud and unearth these slimy treasures.

Worms represent the earth's energy, and they mean someone needs to be grounded. Does your child need to be more settled? Have recent events been overwhelming? Should you just let her go out there in the garden and get dirty for a while? Maybe she feels she is growing up too quickly and just wants to get outside and play.

Farm animals

Pigs

Pigs are viewed with a certain amount of distaste wherever you go. How often have you described your child's untidy room as a pigsty? Or told your child not to be a pig, when he is being greedy?

Has your child been reluctant to tidy up his toys? Has he been gorging himself with sweets and snacks? Moreover, have you been giving him a hard time about it, or has a friend or sibling constantly been pointing it out?

If the pig in your child's dreams isn't reflecting an aspect of his personality, then who else could it be?

Sheep

Sheep are harmless and docile creatures, and their appearance in dreams can that indicate good fortune is on its way.

Aside from that, these white and woolly animals do have a reputation for being easily led. Maybe your child is going along with something instigated by either a sibling or a friend at school, which he knows instinctively is wrong, and it is on his mind. Has he been especially quiet when quizzed about what he has been up to? Many kids follow the lead of an older, more dominant child and are too timid to speak out against the pranks into which they are being drawn. Alternatively, has your child just started to make the connection between real animals and meat? Has he equated the lambs in the field with the food on his plate? Could this be an early pang of vegetarian conscience?

symbolize a person that your child is trying to conquer and bring round to his way of thinking. Have you been particularly resolute about saying no to something your child wants?

Cows

Cows are sacred in Hindu culture, which is probably how the phrase 'holy cow' arose. However, it is more than likely that your child is not aware of the animal's more spiritual connotations and views cows simply as non-threatening, docile creatures which provide the milk that is poured on her cereal every morning.

Your child could associate cows with visits to the countryside, or they may represent a nurturing type of older woman whom the child knows well. Was the cow in her dream happy and contented, or in some sort of distress?

A more traditional interpretation is that cows are a symbol of good fortune and productivity, so perhaps that school project your child has been working on so hard is going to get top marks.

Horses

Depending on their experience of **horses**, most children would not be threatened by our equine friends. Even though as a mode of travel they have been long replaced by the car, horses are still synonymous with adventure. Cowboys and indians, medieval knights, warriors from bygone days have all thundered around on their faithful steeds.

If his dreams feature horses, has your child just started riding lessons, or would he like to? If the dream focuses around falling off a horse, then perhaps this is echoing a real-life situation. Has your child ever had an accident of this type?

Riding a horse is said to represent harnessing life's energy, or the horse can

Bulls

The big question is: has the **bull** in your child's dreams been shown a red flag, and who is waving it? Bulls are associated with anger and the urge to destroy. If the bull is charging at your child, then the chances are that somebody is showing aggression towards her. If the bull is charging at someone else, then your child is feeling very angry towards that person and needs to vent those emotions. Ask her who has been upsetting her so much.

A bull may also represent the blundering characteristics of your child, maybe she has said things without thinking, and has been made aware of this. Have you recently been pointing out this tendency to be a little bit thoughtless?

Chickens

Chickens are commonly associated with cowardice: 'you're a chicken' is an accusation that is flung across the playground from a very early age. Is it possible that your child feels she isn't being brave enough in a certain situation? Could there be some sort of trouble at school that she is too nervous to tell you about? Has someone been pecking away at her, continually jibing and poking fun? Your child may be trying to ignore it to avoid a fight, but perhaps her patience is wearing a little thin.

If your child describes big chickens that are fighting, then she is probably dreaming about cockerels, which are an indication of domestic strife and arguments. Could this be true?

Sea creatures

Fish

Fish represent the spirit of the dreamer, and if your child dreams about fish swimming around in clear water, then he is probably good at expressing his emotions.

The key thing to ask is, how were the fish swimming? If they keep changing direction, then your child is indecisive about something, and perhaps does not know how he feels about some event or person in his life. Also find out what kind of water the fish were swimming in – dark and murky, or clear and calm? The answer to this will give you clues to your child's emotional state.

Alternatively, do you have a pet goldfish or an aquarium or pond? Could your child be dreaming about those?

Dolphins

Dolphins have always carried very special connotations. The ancient Greeks saw them as spiritual guides and messengers, and nowadays many people swim with dolphins as a healing experience. It has also been said that if a child keeps dreaming of dolphins, it could mean that he is spiritually quite gifted.

For some children, their only contact with dolphins is what they see on the television, read about in books or experience at a water park, where these fascinating creatures perform tricks and interact with humans. For others, dolphins are seen every day around the coastline. Dolphins are invariably portrayed in a positive manner and exhibit qualities such as intelligence and friendliness.

These animals tend to appear in dreams when a child is anxious, preoccupied or nervous about a journey. Quite often your child will dream that he is swimming with a dolphin, which acts as a trusted guide in the deep water and is there to save him should anything go wrong. Subconsciously, your child is asking you to do the same. Perhaps it is exam time, or a first school trip without you. Whatever the reason for your child's anxiety, what he needs now is some extra guidance and reassurance.

Sharks

Sharks with their sharp teeth represent the chilling depths of the sea, the hidden dangers that lurk below. What kind of deep, dark emotions are waiting to 'snap up' your child? Could it be that he is feeling angry towards someone at the moment? Or is there anybody around who might be that shark just waiting to attack?

It is time to take a close look at what could be making your child feel threatened, or that might be bringing up negative emotions such as anger or jealousy – unless, of course, he has been watching shark movies, in which case even the bravest of us would be having nightmares.

Whales

Whales are similar to dolphins, in that they have strong spiritual associations. In Native American tradition they represent ancient truths and are known as the 'record keepers' who carry the collective memory of mankind.

These huge creatures are soothing and calming, and can be interpreted as mother figures – perhaps there is a link to a pregnancy?

Their appearance in a dream also reflects maternal warmth, so a few long hugs could be in order.

Monsters

Dragons

Dragons are mythical creatures that have long been part of childhood fantasy. Saint George had to slay the dragon to protect his princess, while the whole imagery of dragons has been kept very much alive in Chinese culture. Is there a dragon that your child wants to fight? Does she feel she has to protect someone from an unpleasant character? Maybe she sees her parent's new partner as a threat.

If there is a fire-breathing dragon in the dream, then maybe someone has been 'breathing fire' in your child's direction. Has she been told off lately?

Has somebody shouted at her?

Dragons can symbolize inner fears that are not totally understood, so perhaps your child doesn't really realize the impact that her bad behaviour may have had. In this case, a quiet chat is necessary.

Dinosaurs

Dinosaurs feature widely in children's books and films. Even though these creatures are long gone, their impact lives on. Does your child fully understand that they lived millions of years ago, or have films like *Jurassic Park* given her the impression that one could be lurking behind the nearest bush?

Dinosaurs can be representative of deeply rooted, overpowering fears, as well as fascination with something that is both dangerous and awe inspiring. Does this sound plausible?

Aliens

Aliens from outer space are a major preoccupation with many children. For some, they are humorous creations that are based on their favourite cartoon characters; for others, they are the evil beings in series such as *Star Trek*, whose sole aim is to wreak havoc on the universe.

If your child dreams that she has been abducted by aliens, then there is an underlying fear of changing surroundings or of losing her home and family. It is important to correlate the aliens with the rest of the dream to try to gauge your child's deepest fears.

Monsters

Monsters come in all shapes and sizes and their favourite hiding places are in cupboards, under the bed and just outside the window. All it takes for a child to conjure up a monster is the dark and a few unrecognizable sounds.

These creatures represent your child's personal demons and could mean that she is running away from something she doesn't want to face. It might be a situation such as bullying, or perhaps an emotion such as jealousy. Many kids do not know how to handle the birth of a new sibling, or feel resentment when it is someone else's birthday, and can't understand why they aren't being showered with all the attention and, more importantly, presents. The best answer for the green-eyed monster is to involve your child as fully as possible in the organizing, and this will help her to develop a more generous spirit.

Insects and creepy-crawlies

Wasps and bees

To a child **wasps and bees** look similar, and both will sting if you get too close. In conventional dream interpretations, wasps mean that enemies are close at hand, while bees can have regal connections and be a sign of good fortune. So, either your child has befriended some unsavoury children, or he is about to get an unexpected surprise – perhaps the chance to play the part of a king in the school play?

Essentially both wasps and bees are associated with pain and a warning of some sort. Is your child being 'stung' by something or somebody? Or does he feel that someone is hovering over him?

Flies

Flies equate to bad energy and feelings of envy, jealousy and resentment. Also, they are generally thought to be a bad omen. This is of no surprise as they congregate on animal droppings, contaminate food and buzz in an irritating way. Who or what could be getting to your child and making him feel like lashing out?

On a common-sense note: are you leaving your child's bedroom window open at night? Could it be that the incessant buzzing is coming from outside and disturbing his sleep?

Spiders

Spiders have many different meanings, depending on the context of the dream. Big, black, hairy spiders denote fear, whereas a busy little one spinning a web means that your child's efforts will be reaping rewards. And if a spider is climbing up a wall, all his wishes will come true.

Spiders can also be the symbol of an overpowering woman who has drawn your child into her web.

The most important thing to establish is whether or not your child is scared of spiders. If so, then you should probably go with the first interpretation: fear.

Dream interpretation
People

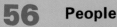

People

People often appear in dreams to represent an aspect of the dreamer. Sometimes it might be a person your child knows, but more often than not it will be an archetypal figure who represents a certain characteristic or quality. This could be a policeman who sends out a message of authority and order, or a mother figure who reflects the caring and feminine side of the dreamer. The dream could also be reflecting real-life issues your child has with the person who appears.

Family and friends

Family

Family issues will often be the major subject matter in children's dreams. Any dream-time conflicts with parents, siblings or even friends have little symbolism other than that these are real-life issues which need to be addressed.

Your child may try to make sense of things he doesn't understand by dreaming of conversations and situations as he would like them to turn out, or as he fear they might. Maybe his dreams are the only place where he has the confidence to say how he really feels. Are there any current traumas or misunderstandings that could be playing on his mind?

If your child dreams of a mother figure, then it could suggest that more nurturing is necessary. If she is telling him off, then he has probably done something wrong, got away with it, and feels guilty.

When dreaming of a father figure, the child will see him in one of two roles: he will either represent protection and security or, if there have been run-ins with his own father lately, the figure will take on a more disciplinarian personality.

If your child dreams of a happy family scene, then he is settled and contented.

Old people

Old people in dreams can mean a multitude of things, all of which depends on each individual child's experience and understanding of his elders. Traditionally signifying wisdom and associated with the more developed part of our minds, they could be carrying important subliminal messages that will help your child deal with an issue in his life. This is particularly true if the old person is someone with whom he is not familiar. Some children seem to be 'old souls': perhaps this could be an example of an ancient inner wisdom helping them in their everyday life.

Is your child worried about an elderly relative or neighbour? Has he just made the connection between getting old and death? The concept of ageing is difficult for a child to comprehend and can reveal itself in a dream as a signal that your child is nervous about the future.

Angels

Angels are a wonderful addition to your child's dreams, signifying that he is feeling protected. They can also be dream messengers, and many children profess to seeing angels in times of crisis who guide them through and give them hope. This is, of course, very much related to the dreamer's beliefs and culture, as 'angels on high' are essentially associated with Christianity.

Nevertheless, if your child tells you he saw an angel, it is wise to ask yourself why he may have summoned up such help, and try to offer the guidance he could be seeking at this time.

Professionals

Doctors

Doctors and dentists mean very different things. To a child, a doctor is someone who will make you better, whereas a dentist is associated more with pain. Their dream interpretations reflect this.

A dream **doctor** is a sort of spirit doctor who will show you symbolically how to rectify a certain situation – how to 'make it better'. What was the doctor saying or showing to your child? Could it be relevant to anything she is going through at the moment? Is there a problem at home or at school?

Dentists

The appearance of a **dentist** means a major crisis is occurring. In fact, any dream involving teeth means that big changes are on their way, particularly if the teeth are falling out. For a child, this could mean no more than growing up, as the loss of the milk teeth is a normal and unavoidable rite of passage.

Doctors and dentists appearing in dreams can also mean that your child really needs to confide in someone, is worried about illness or is simply embarrassed about her bodily functions.

Nurses

If your child dreams about a **nurse**, this suggests that she is in the process of being healed, either physically or emotionally, or is in need of healing and pampering. Now is the time to offer extra reassurance and cuddles.

As with doctors, a dream about a nurse may signify that your child has a need to confide in someone she respects, so make yourself available in case she wants to talk to you about something that is important to her. Again, such a dream may mean that your child is scared of falling ill or is embarrassed about her physical self. Talking through such issues will help her achieve a realistic perspective on her fears.

Teachers

Teachers play an extensive role in the life of every child, and each will have her own relationship with her teacher. For some, the teacher represents a wise, authoritative figure who is trusted and respected; for others, this may not quite be the case. Is your child perhaps afraid of her teacher? Alternatively, the presence of a teacher in her dreams could be more about problems she is having at school.

Taking it a stage further, the teacher could represent the wise self within, manifesting to tell the dreamer something. Maybe your child has made the association between being told to 'do the right thing' and knowing instinctively what that is.

Authority figures

Kings and queens

Kings and queens are romantic figures who are all-powerful and in control. They can represent elements of your child's personality, or be someone he knows who is in a position of authority. They can also represent a child's parents.

A **queen** often symbolizes Mother Nature. Qualities such as a strong sense of equality and fairness are usually associated with a queen. Is she living up to this image in the dream, or behaving more like the wicked stepmother in the tale of Snow White? If the latter is the

case, then there may be problems in the child's relationship with his mother.

The **king** represents a strong will and is often a father figure. But he can also symbolize that your child is struggling with an overly dominant personality, which could be either someone else's or his own. Is his king a kind ruler, or a vile dictator who has people's heads chopped off? This could tell you a lot, either about your child or about the reaction he is experiencing to a male figure in his life – either good or bad.

Soldiers and police officers

Soldiers and police officers are the archetypal keepers of the peace, and for most children in the western world this would be true. But if you live in a country where soldiers and police officers are associated with tyranny, then they are more likely to be symbols of fear.

The **soldier** traditionally represents the brave hero, the person the dreamer would like to be. Is your child the soldier in the dream? What is he fighting for? And against whom? Could there be something your child is feeling passionate about, but not expressing? If there is a lot of fighting going on, then he is struggling between aggressive impulses and the fear of losing control of his emotions.

A **police officer** symbolizes law and order, and can appear in dreams when your child has acted in a way that he knew was wrong. Perhaps your child has a guilty conscience and is scared of being found out? The dream will probably recur

if he does not confess his transgression.

Another way of interpreting why your child has conjured up a police officer in a dream is as a sign that he wants more order or direction in his life. Have you been leaving your child to his own devices, trusting that he will cope on his own? Maybe things like regular times for homework and more structure in his daily life would help.

Heroes and villains

Superheroes

Superheroes represent the ultimate good-guy image for kids, even more so than real figures. Their infiltration into the minds of children is widespread: pick up a cartoon book or watch any children's video or computer game and invariably there will be all-action figures with superhuman powers, fighting for the good of all and annihilating evil forces with a quick blast of their laser gun. What child doesn't want to be blessed with these powers? Imagine flying around the universe and back with Superman – what an incredible dream-time adventure.

Baddies and villains

Baddies and villains represent the other side of the coin: we would have no need for good characters if we did not have their malevolent adversaries. Their appearance in dreams isn't always a bad sign – it can mean that the dreamer is acknowledging a bad trait and dealing with it. The main thing to find out is whether your child was the baddie in question or, conversely, if some villainous character was out to get her.

If a dream features robbers, then maybe your child is feeling insecure. What is someone trying to steal from her?

Witches and vampires

Witches and vampires are the Hallowe'en creatures that frighten most children, but nevertheless they love to dress up as them. If your child is exhibiting extreme fear about either a witch or a vampire, you could buy her the appropriate outfit; this tends to dispel the nightmares, as it gives her back control of her fantasy character.

Traditionally, a **witch** means that there is disenchantment with somebody or strong misgivings about another person. Quite often, a child will conjure up her mother as a witch if there have been a few too many arguments.

Vampires with their sharp, pointed fangs mean your child is feeling slightly threatened and vulnerable. Who could be 'out for her blood'?

Jailers

A **jailer** is the symbol of the dreamer's conscience. If your child tells you that somebody wanted to lock her up, ask her why. Your child is trying to punish herself for past errors, and probably feels guilty about what she did. It may be something you know about, or it could be a secret about which you have no idea. Perhaps she got into trouble at a friend's house and has not told you.

Dream interpretation
Natural World

Natural World

The way in which nature features in your child's dreams can be a great indicator of how he is developing and growing. It can also highlight how he views the immediate world around him, as gardens, forests, fields and beaches are representative of the external environment. We are all linked to nature, and its cycles reflect our own. Interpret natural symbols as a part of your child and you cannot go far wrong.

Forests and trees

Forests

Forests can be frightening places, full of mythical creatures such as fairies and goblins, and home to many wild animals. What hidden dangers lurk behind the trees?

If your child is dreaming of being lost in a forest, it could mean that she is travelling to the depths of her unconscious. Alternatively, this might relate to a real experience.

Wandering through a forest means your child is seeking to find out more about herself. Ask whether it was dark and scary, or if the sun was shining. What did she see there? Could it be that your child is feeling lost, and doesn't know which way to turn? What is it she is so afraid of? Tell her that if she dreams of this again, she should ask for someone to show her the way. A good guide will reveal amazing truths to your child.

Trees

Trees are the universal symbol of life itself and represent growth. They are said to mirror the different stages of human life: the seed is symbolic of the embryo; blossoming and branching out represent youth; maturity is mirrored by the production of fruit or new seeds.

Many religions and cultures use the tree as a symbol of humankind's connection between earth and the heavens. The roots penetrate the ground, while the branches stretch upwards towards the sky. If there is one tree, it signifies either an individual or the family unit.

The type of tree is vital as an indication of how your child feels she is growing. A deciduous or flowering tree is a positive symbol. It means life and vitality – your child is blossoming. An evergreen is a sign of everlasting life, so perhaps your child is more spiritually aware than you realize.

Is it a fruit tree? In that case, your child is happy and productive. Expect glowing school reports.

If the tree is withered, with no leaves on its branches, then your child is lacking something – could it be affection or praise? What can you do to make her feel more nurtured or to bolster her self-confidence?

If the tree is ancient and awe inspiring, then your child could be connecting to a higher universal force, and is starting to learn more about the size and age of the world in which we live.

According to the Buddhist faith, the Buddha became enlightened while he sat under the bodhi tree. Does your child need some time to reflect on recent events or conversations?

Flowers and fruit

Flowers

Flowers play a pivotal role both in nature and in our daily lives. They are universal symbols of beauty, innocence, purity and gentleness. In a dream, they can indicate that developments are about to take place. If they are fresh it is a good sign, but dried or withered flowers mean hopes and dreams are not being fulfilled, or something has happened to darken your child's innocent outlook. Alternatively, he may know people named after flowers, and the flower appears in the dream as a representation of that person.

If your child describes a flower with sharp bits that prickle, then he is probably dreaming about a **rose**. This is, of course, the flower of love, and love can hurt from time to time.

A field of **daisies** with the sun shining means everything is going well. A big yellow flower is probably a **sunflower** and means that your child has a good nature.

If your child has been dreaming of pink flowers, these might be **carnations**, which represent maternal love. Or perhaps he has seen these flowers in a wedding bouquet.

Even though they don't hold quite the same morbid connotations as they once used to, **lilies** could signify some sort of connection with a death. Possibly there has been a funeral or loss recently, and your child has taken certain images away with him.

Poppies, with their deep red colour, could have something to do with the image of blood. Have you been getting out the first aid box to deal with grazed knees lately?

Fruit

Fruit can represent something coming to fruition, someone reaping the fruits of their labours. Has your child been working hard to achieve something, or saving up his pocket money to buy a long-awaited treat?

What fruit is it that he describes in his dreams? **Apples** are a sign of good health – remember the saying 'an apple a day keeps the doctor away' – but **blackberries** are associated with darker forces, and their brambles and thorns will stand in the way of happiness. Could it be that your child feels that something is still out of his grasp? Maybe he needs that extra little bit of encouragement to help him achieve his goals.

If your child was eating the fruit in his dream, ask if it was sweet or bitter. This will show you whether or not he feels his effort was worth it in the end.

Landscapes

Mountains

Mountains are regarded as obstacles and are associated with goals in life that have to be attained. For a child, this could be a test at school or a trial for a sports team.

The way in which your child is rising to these challenges is indicated by where she is on the mountain. If she is at the bottom, this indicates that she is overwhelmed by what lies ahead; at the top, and she feels she is succeeding and achieving results.

Spiritually, events that take place on a mountain are always of great importance. It is a place where one becomes 'conscious'.

Fields

Fields and countryside are said to be a sign of good times ahead, but think carefully about what these places might mean to your child. Do you live in this kind of environment? Is it somewhere you walk the dog, or where the children play? Or is it a place that is visited only occasionally, as you live in an urban area? If so, could your child be crying out for a bit of space and peace?

The naturalness and beauty of the countryside has particular relevance to hobbies and creative pursuits, so perhaps your child needs more freedom in order to express herself on that level.

If none of this seems to apply, then rest assured that being surrounded by beautiful countryside is a sign that all is well and your child is contented. However, if the landscape is barren then the reverse is probably true.

Gardens

Gardens represent your child's external environment and how she feels about it at that particular moment in time. For instance, if a garden is overgrown and in disarray, then she is confused and overwhelmed by circumstances.

Gardens can also reveal a lot about your child's temperament. A very tidy, formal garden symbolizes someone who is extremely organized and possibly predictable, so you shouldn't be confronted by many surprises. This is a child who likes to know that everything is in the right place. If the garden is sprawling, then she is probably an effusive character who takes each day as it comes.

If your child describes a garden full of flowers, this a positive symbol. In the same way that plants and trees emerge, grow and develop, positive changes are taking place in her life. Everything in her garden is 'rosy'.

At the seaside

The sea and beaches

The **sea and beaches** can have many associations for a child. Perhaps he is looking forward to a trip to the seaside, or re-living a previous holiday. Dreaming of a beach where the water is calm generally means that everything in your child's life is calm, and that he has a secure frame of mind. If the sea is turbulent with big waves, then there is emotional unrest.

On a primordial level, we all came from the water. All life started here, so it is an old symbol of fertility, life and renewal. The emotions are strongly linked with water, so use these images to assess the ebb and flow of your child's feelings.

Mud and stones

From an adult perspective, **mud and stones** do not have positive dream interpretations. **Mud** can indicate major difficulties: phrases such as 'stuck in the mud' or 'wading through mud', are used to describe feelings of frustration when nothing seems to be moving fast enough or you are dealing with a person who won't move on an issue.

For a small child, mud is great fun. You can dig it, make mud pies with it, find all sorts of interesting things in it. The only bad aspect is when you are made to wash because you are filthy. So, possibly a better way to interpret mud in a child's dream is to look for what your youngster might be trying to wash away. Could it be a guilty secret or negative experience?

Stones conjure up connotations such as cold, hard and strong, and are associated with a cold heart and lack of compassion. Could it be that a person with a 'heart of stone' is playing on your child's mind?

Are plans that have been 'set in stone' frustrating your child because he wants to do something else, or is he feeling reassured because someone in his life is 'as solid as a rock'?

Caves

Caves represent the inner realms, the unconscious. If a child dreams about a cave, then some aspect of his character is waiting to be discovered or is hidden away during everyday life.

If the cave was very dark and scary, then the chances are that your child was frightened to go there – perhaps it is the home of a ferocious bear or writhing snake? Did a monster leap out and scare him?

If these terrifying characters were preventing your child from reaching the buried treasure hidden deep in the cave, then fear is probably holding him back from exploring his potential and discovering hidden gifts. It is time for some encouragement.

Metals and minerals

Metals and minerals come in a wide variety of shapes and sizes, and have many different meanings in dreams. They can be practical, such as pots and pans, or symbols of treasure, such as precious jewels. It is always wise to take not only the metal or mineral into consideration, but also the object into which it has been fashioned.

Iron

Iron is the symbol of strong will, endurance and a powerful sense of purpose. Is this being tested? Perhaps your child is learning to ride a bicycle or is determined to perfect a skill, such as playing a musical instrument.

Brass

Brass signifies good luck and is traditionally associated with money. If your child is dreaming of lots of coins, maybe there is about to be an extra bonus in her pocket money.

Crystals

Crystals are made up of minerals that are thought to have been created at the same time as the universe. They were used by many ancient civilizations for spiritual illumination and healing – and many people today use them for this purpose, so it is quite possible that your child has come into contact with them.

Crystals are also a sign of delicate emotions and fragility. What type of crystal is your youngster dreaming about? This could be her way of telling you what emotional support she feels she is lacking.

Purple crystals are probably **amethyst**, which is associated with spiritual healing and calming. It also aids the transition from wakefulness to sleep.

Clear crystals would be **quartz**, which amplifies energy and gives vitality and strength. If placed under the pillow, it is said to help the dreamer communicate with higher sources.

Pink crystals are **rose quartz**, the crystal that symbolizes love and can help if someone feels sad or lonely.

Yellow crystals are **citrine**, which is used to release fear, or **tiger's eye**, which is said to protect against evil. Citrine is also believed to stimulate the dream process.

There are many more types of crystal, each with their own meaning. If your child regularly dreams of crystals it is a good idea to buy her one of her own. This would be a 'dream gift' that could make her feel safe and protected against nightmares.

Gemstones

Gemstones can symbolize many things, as each has its own meaning and history. They could also possibly relate to someone your child knows who wears a piece of jewellery that contains a certain gemstone.

As there is usually a multitude of different-coloured stones flowing out of a treasure casket in adventure stories, children soon learn the worth of precious gemstones. However, their association with the higher elements of the human psyche is more to do with the qualities they represent than the cost of buying one.

Clear white **diamonds** are a very positive sign when they appear in dreams. This gem symbolizes great inner value and childish innocence.

Deep green **emeralds** mean that your child is feeling well loved and assured of success.

Rich red **rubies** are a sign of great contentment and happiness.

Bright blue **sapphires** indicate that nothing is clouding your child's judgement, as they are the symbol of a clear thinker.

Dream interpretation
Special Occasions and Events

Special Occasions and Events

Every event has its own unique symbolism, as each represents a pivotal moment or stage in a person's life. The feelings associated with each event are personal and vary from individual to individual, and when they occur in your child's dreams it is these feelings and associations for which you should be looking.

Rites of passage

Death

Death is symbolic of change, and in a dream it usually denotes the end of an important phase, to be followed by a rebirth of some kind. However difficult the circumstances, an adult can usually understand this concept. For a child, it may represent fear of change, sometimes played out as the death of one or both parents, reflecting her ultimate fear that her parents may leave for ever.

If a beloved person has recently died and a child dreams about this, it has emotional rather than symbolic meaning.

Sometimes dreams about death can mean that the dreamer has had a painful experience and feels badly hurt.

Look at your child's understanding and experience of death, and the surrounding circumstances at the time of the dream. It may be that it simply represents change, and that your child has to 'bury' a conflict, a friendship, even a way of life, and make room for the new. Life is cyclical, and even though falling out with her best friend may be painful, reassure her that she will soon make new friends.

Birth

Birth has similar connotations to death, in that it represents the birth of something new – whether this is an idea, a friendship or even a new sibling. It can be that obvious. Is your child about to have a new brother or sister? If this is the case, what was the nature of the dream? Did it give any hint of fear, or was it a happy dream?

If there is no birth imminent, then this kind of dream symbolizes a new start for your child and is a good omen for the future.

Marriage

Marriage signifies the union of compatible opposites, joining together to form a whole. It can also mean that a mystical marriage of the soul is taking place, and a new level of understanding is being reached.

If your child is attending a wedding in the dream, this means that good news is on the way or, more obviously, that she is actually about to go to a wedding!

Another possible interpretation is that there is some domestic friction going on, and this is your child's way of asking you to resolve things.

Divorce and separation

Divorce and separation dreams are often based on a child's fear or experience of such a reality. In this case, your child will need all the reassurance and understanding you can muster. It may be that she has misunderstood something when she overheard an argument between you and your partner, or has heard friends talking about their parents splitting up.

Such a dream can also indicate a forced change or split ideals. Do you want your child to do her homework the minute she comes in from school, while she feels she should be allowed to play for a while? Maybe there is some kind of compromise to be reached.

Celebration

Birthdays

Birthdays are constantly on the minds of young children, whose entire existence seems to be caught up in a whirl of friends' birthday parties and, of course, their own. So, if their dreams are a mixture of birthday cakes and games, this is pure enjoyment and excitement.

If your child is dreaming of being late for his own party, or of nobody showing up, this is a sign of anxiety and a fear of being unpopular.

Christmas

Christmas is a sign of good fortune in a dream, and usually represents the same things as a birthday. The major thought on your child's mind is, 'Will I get a new bike or computer?' This in itself can produce some anxiety.

One thing to consider is that if your child has ever had a negative experience around Christmas-time, this may cause bad dreams.

If your child dreams about Christmas Eve, this may be a sign that he is always waiting for something good to happen.

Parades and carnivals

Parades and carnivals can mean that not all is well, particularly if your child is watching. This can symbolize that life is passing him by, and may mean that he wants to be involved with things, but is too shy or reserved to push himself forward. He may feel that he is continually being passed over: does your child come home from school with tales of woe because he wasn't chosen for the football team – again – or that nobody ever seems to want him on their side? Perhaps he would love to get up in class and read his poem, but is too shy to put his hand up.

Also check if everyone in the parade or carnival was masked. This reveals that your child is feeling great distrust of those around him as masks conceal the truth or hide faults behind the guise of superficial attractiveness or feigned sincerity.

Theatre

Watching a theatre performance is the mind 'acting out' thoughts and feelings. Your child has created a scenario in his head that he either wishes would happen or suspects is happening, and he may be trying to direct the outcome.

What was the nature of the performance, and who were the major players? Does it sound like anything that could be based in reality?

Perhaps your child feels that things are going on around him over which he has no control; possibly he feels left on the outside of events that are taking place.

Stressful situations

Winning and losing are strong themes in dreams and detail how your child feels about certain situations.

Winning

Dreaming of **winning** a race or a competition could be prophetic, and might reflect your child's drive and ambition. Many sportsmen and women have said that in the build-up to winning an important championship they have dreamed of holding the trophy or medal in their hands.

Conversely, it may be that your child is too nervous even to enter in real life, and these dreams are therefore exactly that – merely a dream. If this is the case, then you need to help her overcome her lack of self-confidence.

Losing

Losing can denote that great changes are about to happen, or that your child is exhibiting a fear of failure. Reassure her that she should just try her best.

Sometimes the interpretation can be more obvious. If your youngster dreams of losing a watch, perhaps she feels that she is running out of time – or maybe you should check your jewellery box!

Exams

Examination dreams usually indicate that your child feels inadequately prepared for a certain situation, which could be either an exam or some scenario in which she feels she is being tested. Could she feel that your expectations of her are too high?

Holidays

Holidays in dreams mean exactly that: it is time to take a break. Is your child getting excited about an imminent holiday or, alternatively, is she feeling pressurized? Is there too much crammed into her life at the moment, such as one too many after-school clubs? Or has it been a particularly stressful time at home? Many people don't even consider that a child needs time to relax and unwind, but as active as they seem, it can all come crashing down in exactly the same way as with adults.

Has your child been complaining lately of being tired, or having sleeping problems? Do you have to drag her out of bed in the mornings, and has she been catching every minor infection that is going around the playground? Your child may need something to look forward to, and might want to escape to a more relaxed environment.

Moving house

Moving house in a dream could be based on reality, particularly if your child is starting to be surrounded by packing cases and is having to say goodbye to friends and teachers.

It can also be symbolic of the need to bring about change in your youngster's life, whether to her image, attitude, frame of mind, environment or behaviour.

The classic 'my parents moved and left me behind' dream is a sign that your child has a fear of being abandoned, or is feeling insecure at the moment.

So, is your child feeling slightly sad and vulnerable, or is she maybe bored?

Actions

Actions do speak louder than words. What your child is doing in a dream reflects how he is responding to events in his day-to-day life: is he facing up to things or running away? They can also be symbolic of how your child is making his way through his own journey of life.

Walking

Walking is a symbol of making your way through life. The meaning is completely dependent on where the dreamer is walking. Uphill shows life is a struggle; a narrow lane indicates that something has to be faced soon and there is no escape – is that school project is due in tomorrow?

If your child is walking through open fields with the sun shining, then all is well in his life at the moment. But if he describes somewhere dark and overwhelming, then he may be facing life with trepidation for some reason.

Running

Running suggests that your child is in a hurry either to get somewhere or to get away from something he can't face.

What is he running towards? Is it something he is looking forward to? Maybe he is getting excited about a holiday, or seeing a favourite aunt or uncle.

If he is running away from something, this has the same connotations as being chased – something is behind him, but what?

Chasing

Chasing and being chased shows inner conflict in the dreamer. He is either running away from his worries, or is chasing after that which eludes him. This dream represents the angry, unexpressed self. Being chased by an animal means that the dreamer is running away from his basic instincts – whatever is pursuing your child is a part of his own character. Anger, jealousy, fear and even love can all assume the appearance of something threatening.

In such dreams, a child will often flee and wake up in fear. What could be bothering him so much that he needs to get away? Does he believe he is in a no-win situation? Is he feeling hostile towards a school friend or sibling? Could he be angry because he feels someone is taking advantage of him?

Whatever it is, you need to resolve it, as the problem your child is running away from can take over and dominate his whole life. Encourage him to turn and face the menace, and overcome it in the dream. This is be a good time to call in a 'dream friend' for some extra assistance.

If your child is doing the chasing, what is it he is after? Could it be affection or praise?

Fighting

Fighting in a dream suggests mental conflict, quite often with an aspect of the dreamer's own personality. Your child may want to do something that he knows he shouldn't, and is wrestling with his conscience. Maybe his friends have suggested skipping school and going to the park? Perhaps he wants some extra money to buy sweets on the way to school and knows where you keep your loose change? Whatever the reason, the dream means that your child does not know which way to turn. Just tell him that if he does the right thing, the bad dream will go away.

Jumping

Jumping off something suggests that your child needs to escape from a problem. Look carefully at the rest of the dream to see what else is involved, and also take note of what it is she was jumping off.

If she is jumping onto something, this means she is very eager to be included in an occasion or event and perhaps feels that she is being left behind.

If your child is jumping over things, these represent obstacles that can be overcome, so examine exactly what they are.

On a practical level, is your child involved in trampolining at school, is she learning how to jump into a swimming pool, or has she just started to get involved with athletics? There could be a very simple interpretation.

Playing

Playing is a huge part of children's lives and it makes sense for it to feature in dreams. Your child may describe playing with a favourite toy or cartoon character; she may fantasize about playing with a fellow pupil who as yet isn't a friend; she might be off playing tennis with a top player. It is all pure imagination – an extended form of playtime.

Only worry if she is continually dreaming that she has no one to play with, as this could be the same in real life.

Climbing

Climbing dreams can vary in meaning, depending on what the dreamer is climbing. A mountain means that problems seem insurmountable or that your child is exaggerating their importance. In contrast, a ladder indicates that she is moving up the ladder of success.

Is life an uphill struggle for your child regarding schoolwork? Have results been consistently poor, no matter how much extra effort and hard work she has put in? Are you or your child's teachers bringing this to her attention? Could your youngster be feeling pressured and useless? It is time to highlight the skills that your child does have – this will increase her self-confidence and have a positive impact on the areas where things don't come quite as easily.

Crying

Crying or getting upset in a dream will often be accompanied by real tears. These are tears that need to be shed, so why has your child been biting her lip? Does she need to overcome certain obstacles? Has there been a period of domestic strife, disputes and arguments?

Quite often, an extra-sensitive child will feel that she shouldn't add to what is already going on, because she doesn't want to upset anybody further. This may seem an honourable trait, but it is one that should not be allowed to continue. Your child could carry this through the rest of her life, always believing that her feelings are secondary to those of others.

Falling

Falling in dreams is very common and can be simply the physical sensation of 'falling' asleep. It is not unusual to have an involuntary muscle spasm, and the sudden jerk or falling sensation is simply the muscles relaxing.

On the emotional side, falling can indicate a sense of loss of control. Maybe things that are going on in your child's life are imposing limitations on him, or perhaps someone else is always in the driving seat – do any overly bossy friends spring to mind? Could it be time for your child to start asserting himself? Perhaps you could look for a friend for him who is willing to do what he wants from time to time.

Flying

Flying can mean a mixture of things. Your child may report that he was flying above your house, or buzzing around the world way up in the clouds. It could be the influence of stories, such as Peter Pan or his latest idol who flies from one adventure to another, but it may signify something deeper.

Flying can be a sign of ambition, and if this is the case you should take careful note of how easy the flight was. If in the dream your child was continually having to overcome various obstacles that were obstructing his path, then the same is probably true of real life. What things or people could be standing in the way of his dreams?

Flying can also be a metaphor that shows your child has the ability to rise above problems and cope with whatever comes his way. This is a great attribute.

If you take a more spiritual viewpoint, then it may be that your child's spirit temporarily left his body and took off on an astral flight.

Whatever seems the most appropriate interpretation, flying in dreams leaves the dreamer feeling positive and is never something to be feared.

Frozen

Being frozen with fear, unable to move, can also have a physical explanation. When your child is in REM sleep, his muscles will be flaccid; if he then wakes up, he may not be able to move for a while as his body regains consciousness.

Alternatively, this is a classic anxiety dream. It can mean that your child is unwilling to make changes, or is feeling frustrated and powerless. Maybe he has seen something on the news that has made him realize that bad things might happen to his loved ones, over which he will have no control. Perhaps he is focusing his anxiety on imaginary situations, or has something in his life made him feel this way?

Performing

Dancing

Dancing within a dream can mean that a meeting is about to happen which will change your child's life. This is the most traditional interpretation; on the other hand, it could simply mean that you have a future ballet dancer who is so obsessed with dancing that she even pirouettes in her sleep. Dancing is essentially a happy sign, unless your child constantly dreams of dancing alone, in which case her dreams and aspirations are not being realized. What can you do to help?

Singing

Singing can mean there is a higher source of help around to assist you with any problems that may appear. But if the idea of choirs of angels doesn't appeal, then ask yourself how many times have you caught your child miming in front of the mirror with a hairbrush?

Maybe she is obsessed with a pop

group and dreams of appearing on a big stage in front of a huge audience. This is a childish fantasy that many adults never outgrow, and if the dreams are pleasant and your child is having fun, then the dream is harmless.

On stage/acting

As Shakespeare said, 'All the world's a stage, and all the men and women merely players'. What private thoughts is your child trying to act out when she dreams of being on stage? Or does she actually aspire to being a performer? Alternatively, is she nervous of being **on stage**, and this is more of a nightmare than a dream?

Why would your child feel that she is under scrutiny and everyone is watching? Or could she be testing out hidden aspects of her personality? Who is the audience and what is their reaction? This will tell you how comfortable your child is with this side of her character. If there is no audience, then your child is probably a very private person, who perhaps lives in her own fantasy land from time to time. Is there anything in her world which could cause her to want to escape?

Performing in a circus

If your child dreams that she is a **circus performer**, this can tell you many things, depending on the nature of the performance. If she is a clown, then all is not well and she is putting on a brave face. If she is juggling balls or hoops and keeps dropping them, she probably feels that she is trying to deal with too many things at once and isn't coping very well.

But if your child is in the ring or a cage with wild animals, then she feels that she is in some sort of danger. What kind of pressure could she be under at the moment?

Water world

Swimming

Swimming is associated with the emotions, and can indicate that the dreamer is feeling 'bathed in emotion'. Is this a particularly turbulent time for your child? In the dream, did he have to swim hard to stay afloat? Is he feeling like a 'fish out of water' in a particular situation? What was the water like? If he was swimming in a pool, this indicates frustration and lack of self-expression. Or was he having a lovely swim in calm water? If this is the case, there is no need to worry.

More practically, perhaps your child has been having swimming lessons and has recently mastered his first stroke.

Drowning

Drowning usually means that the dreamer is being engulfed by major problems.

If your child's head rises above water or he is rescued in the dream, then he is capable of dealing with everything.

Because water represents the emotions, the dreamer is likely to be emotionally low. Is it possible that your child is getting things out of perspective?

Or could this dream be linked to a real-life bad experience connected to water? Has he ever gone under and had difficulty in getting back to the surface – perhaps fallen into a pool or tripped in the bath? It only takes one mishap for a child to re-live it time and time again.

Urinating

Urinating in a dream can precede or accompany actual bedwetting. If this is the case, then you need to employ the usual tactics of restricting fluid intake and waking up your child periodically to enable him to empty his bladder. Are you trying to toilet train your child and having difficulties?

On a psychological level, dreaming of urinating represents the need to let go. What could this be? It may be that he is hanging on to an element of childhood, showing resistance to growing up and becoming more independent. Is this accompanying going to school and being separated from a parent or carer for the first time?

Looking for the toilet

As with urinating, **looking for the toilet** in a dream can mean that your child actually needs to pass water. It also suggests that he needs to find a private place where he can get rid of pent-up emotions that are difficult to express in real life.

If your youngster says that in the dream he had to go to the toilet in front of other people, this means that he is self-conscious and worried about what other people think of him.

Dream interpretation
Elements

Elements

These natural phenomena represent the emotions and feelings of your child. She may feel as if she is drowning in a certain situation, wants to explode with anger or needs to shed a little light on something that she doesn't understand. These are very important aspects of the dream to establish, as they provide the essential information you need in order to gauge your child's emotional state.

The natural cycle

Daytime dreams

Daytime dreams – or rather, dreams set in daylight – are all about present situations and feelings. Your child knows how he feels and may just be trying to make sense of a situation or re-live an experience and enjoy it all over again. There is clarity in your child's life: everything is better in the light of day.

Night-time dreams

Night-time dreams indicate that your child feels he is 'in the dark' or doesn't understand something. There could be fear, or a crisis of some kind. Maybe he is concealing resentment – what is there that needs to be brought into the light?

This type of dream could just be an extension of being afraid of the dark, so perhaps your child is blurring reality with the dream. If there are a moon and stars in it, that is a better omen as it signifies wholeness and peace.

Seasons – Spring

Spring is the universal symbol of new ideas and rebirth. If your child has had a tough time lately, then a dream about the spring is a reminder that he can make a fresh start and overcome even the most difficult circumstances.

Subconsciously, such a dream can be a prompt to start something new. Maybe your child is on a creative high: has he spent a lot of time recently drawing or making things?

Summer

Summer settings are associated with relaxation, cloudless skies, vibrant colour and warmth. Dreams with this theme represent satisfaction, tranquillity and contentment. Your child should be in a happy frame of mind at the moment.

Has he just done particularly well in a test or exam, or been selected for a school sports team? Summer dreams mean the dreamer feels they have achieved something – so maybe your child could do with a break from the usual routine.

Autumn

Autumn leaves falling can indicate a sense of time running out and sadness at the end of an era. It is also the season of the harvest, so perhaps it is time for the dreamer to reap what he has sown.

Has your child been talking in 'if only' terms recently? Is there anything he may be regretting and wishing he had done another way? Maybe that school project was completed in a rush at the last minute.

Winter

Winter signifies great success or a time for quiet and rest. It is time to snuggle up on the sofa and indulge in comfort food. This season symbolizes hibernation time, and maybe a withdrawal into oneself for a little introspection. Does your child need some time to rest and reflect? Has life been hectic lately?

Winter in a dream can also mean boredom, so perhaps not enough has been going on recently and your child feels he has been hibernating and is desperate to get out and become involved.

Sky and flame

Sky

They say the **sky** is the limit. Does your child have lofty goals and ambitions? Are you looking at a future class prefect? Or is she aiming to be published in the school magazine?

Are there **clouds** in the sky? This could mean that your child is feeling gloomy and depressed. It could also be symbolic of a pessimistic nature. Is something standing in the way of her desires?

Conversely, if there are beautiful, billowing white clouds set against a bright blue sky, this denotes contentment, optimism and a sense that anything she tries will end in success.

So, is your child resolutely cheerful even when things look bleak, or is it a case of always thinking the worst? Perhaps you ought to help your natural-born worrier find a few silver linings in those grey clouds.

Fire

Fire is a many-sided symbol. On the positive side, fire provides warmth and light to illuminate the path of life and can represent the emotional security of the family home. Could your child be asking for some help from you because she is a bit confused at the moment and needs some reassurance and guidance? Is it possible that she is trying to understand previously hidden aspects of her personality?

On the negative side, fire can be all-consuming and represent powerful emotions such as desire and hate. Terms such as 'burning with desire' and 'fuelled by passion' use fire as a symbol of emotion. If the fire is out of control, the emotions are, too. How big and rampaging is this fire?

Fire can also have a very constructive meaning, symbolizing the destruction of old ideas and feelings that no longer have relevance. In this instance, fire is a symbol of purification: the old is destroyed to make way for the new.

Volcanoes

A **volcano** could indicate that an explosive situation is on the way. This is a loud and clear warning of building tension.

Volcanoes often symbolize violent feelings and thoughts. These feelings may not be those of your child but could easily be representative of a temperamental person in her life. The rest of the dream is very important if you want to decipher the meaning of this symbol.

The heavens

Sun

'The **sun** has got its hat on and is coming out to play' – let's hope it is in your child's dream, because a sun that is shining brightly means that he is happy, contented and full of great hopes for the future. It is seen as the giver of life and sustenance. If it is sunny, then hopefully your child does not want for anything.

The sun also symbolizes insight and male energy. Which male character is having a positive impact on your child's life at the moment? This could be a father, brother, or possibly a male teacher.

If your child is dreaming of a **rising sun**, then a new phase is about to start or a new idea about to happen. Something is dawning on him. If there has been unrest, then this dream could be a welcome reminder that every new day brings with it the possibility that things will get better.

If the **sun is setting**, then the opposite is true: a phase is over, or your child is running out of time to complete something. Would you say that he is the sort of child who is always starting things but never finishing them?

A sun that is partially hidden by clouds means that whatever the current problems are, they are only temporary, and your child has the ability to see ahead of them and know that everything will be fine in the end.

Moon

The **moon** is feminine and linked with emotions and maternal matters. It is also a symbol of peace and harmony. Perhaps your child is in need of some mothering and nurturing.

Was the moon in the dream full or crescent-shaped? If full, then your child is due a period of intense happiness; if crescent or half-moon, then there could be some mental confusion about something.

The moon is also linked with romance, so your child may be in the throes of his first 'crush'. Has he been begging you to buy posters of a particular pop star, or is there somone he likes at school?

Stars

The **stars** are associated with many things. A five-pointed star, or pentagram, is supposed to protect people from witch-craft and evil. The six-pointed star, or Star of David, is the symbol of the Jewish faith and represents the six days of creation. It is a sign of peace and hope, and can also indicate self-confidence and destiny. Is your child destined for greatness?

Stars in the sky can prophesy the birth of a baby – perhaps your child knows something you don't!

Stormy weather

Rain

Rain means that troubles need to be washed away – the heavier the rain, the greater the problem. Are the dreams of spring showers or a monsoon? Rain is symbolic of tears and sadness, so this indicates that your child is trying to find a way to release unshed tears. But this can also be healthy, as the rain washes away the dust, clears the air, and can make what was once arid land fertile once more. Maybe she is ready to begin again and make a new start.

If your child describes being stuck indoors while the rain pours down outside, then has somebody dampened her enthusiasm for something? Alternatively, does she always put everything off because of external factors?

Storms

Storms are a warning of trouble on the horizon. Does your child have good reason to feel a sense of foreboding? A storm is symbolic of powerful, pent-up emotions that are waiting to boil over. Perhaps your child is particularly stressed at the moment and needs to release her frustrations or repressed anger. It could even be that your child is so frightened at the strength of her feelings that, by conjuring up a storm in her dreams, she has created a safe, socially acceptable image, rather than lose control in reality.

Thunder and lightning

Thunder and lightning are a powerful warning and seek to bring enlightenment and understanding. Many children are petrified of these phenomena, so is this the case with your child? Or should you be trying to work out just what it is that she is doing, despite being told not to? There could be a strong fixation with that hot stove or the forbidden cupboard that is full of things she shouldn't touch.

Lightning is generally a more positive symbol than thunder, which warns of impending disaster. Flashes of lightning are there to illuminate something in the dream – the question is, what? It could be a person or scene that the dreamer needs to understand more about. If your child is instinctively wary and cautious, these dreams could represent 'flashes of insight'.

Rainbows

Rainbows are a sign of hope, good fortune and luck. After all, at the end of the rainbow is a pot of gold. It could also show that your child could need a bit of magic and mystery in her life. How about a surprise trip, or even a treasure hunt?

Cold weather

Wind

Changes are on the way if your child is dreaming of the **wind**. This is a sign of having to face up to something. The type of wind reflects the severity of the situation: a light breeze is a little nudge in the right direction, whereas a Force Nine gale where everything is destroyed suggests that this inevitable change should happen as soon as possible. What could your child be procrastinating about?

Was the wind frightening? Was your child being blown along? Did he feel completely out of control? There may be some fear of change present, because even though he knows that a move or change in his situation is inevitable, he is reluctant to leave all that is familiar and secure behind. This could be related to starting at a new school, or are you moving house?

Fog

Fog or mist in a dream can be a sign of an introverted personality. It can also mean that the dreamer can't or won't see what is right in front of him. The truth is hidden because it is difficult to deal with, or someone has been misleading him. Has your child suffered some loss of direction lately, perhaps falling in with a bad crowd?

Or could it be that something traumatic has happened in the past, and he has put a screen over it to try to banish the memory? Find out if your child had any idea as to what could have been hidden in the fog. Ask him to close his eyes and imagine it melting away. What can he see now?

Snow and ice

Snow and ice are both signs of emotional coldness and lack of feelings. They can also indicate that someone involved is rigid in his way of thinking. Has anything happened to make your child numb his feelings, or is somebody in his life displaying these characteristics?

What situation has your child put on ice because he can't deal with it at the moment, and what can you do to try to start the thaw?

A trail of footprints in the snow means that your child secretly admires someone and would almost like to be them, or 'follow in their footsteps'.

Alternatively, have you just come back from a skiing holiday, had a white Christmas, or enjoyed building a snowman in the garden? Once again, personal associations are extremely important to interpretation.

Dream interpretation
Places

Places

Places are part of the fabric of our lives that hold many memories and evoke special feelings. For a child, the home could represent a place of security and peace, but it might just as easily be the scene of domestic unrest and family squabbles. Try to imagine how your child feels in certain environments and work out why this is a place she has to return to in her dreams.

Home

Houses

The house is the mansion of the soul, or the representation of the body. It is often a composite of all the houses the dreamer has ever known, which in the case of a small child may be very few. But essentially it represents the dreamer, as they see themselves, or wish to be seen. There are several thing to look out for. What is the condition of the house – is it run down? This could indicate poor health. Is it empty? Is it in a peaceful location? Does it remind you of anywhere in particular?

If it is a **huge mansion**, this doesn't necessarily mean that your child has grandiose illusions about himself. It is more likely that he is feeling a little unsettled at the moment, and that the dozens of unexplored rooms are feelings and memories that he is avoiding facing up to.

To dream of **building a house** often

means that there are big changes afoot, and that the dreamer has maximum self-confidence.

Rooms

Individual rooms can all represent different meanings. The **kitchen** is often the centre of family life and, depending on the nature of the dream, this will indicate whether or not there is harmony in the family. Look at the state of the kitchen and ask about the atmosphere – this will reveal your child's current attitude to family and friends.

If the room is deserted, then your child feels there isn't enough closeness in the family, or maybe nobody is willing to share emotions and feelings.

If the place is littered with half-eaten meals, then there is building tension within the family and no one is airing their problems.

But if the kitchen seems cosy, with plenty of food and family activity, then all is well and your child is feeling nourished in every sense of the word.

The **bathroom** is where you wash and scrub, so there may be a need to wash away fears or troubles. It is also a very private place, so it could be that a few secrets are being kept. Have you noticed that your child has been feeling vulnerable lately? Perhaps there have been a few more teary outbursts than usual? This may take a lot of patience and sensitivity on your part, but your child needs to talk.

A **bedroom** can indicate that a period of ill-health is due, and your child may need some rest and relaxation. Unconsciously, he is realizing the need to escape the stress of his waking life, which could mean that there are problems at school or at home. This is a time to gather strength, so make sure your child gets his vitamins regularly.

Forbidding buildings

Castles and fortresses

Like a house, **a castle or fortress** is also seen as the mansion of the soul, but a more powerful version. They can indicate that your child feels physically under siege, or needs more freedom. Have you had to ground her recently? If your child is the one laying siege, then she is battling against someone much stronger, possibly an older child or parent. If the castle is empty or abandoned, then she needs to rest, and take a break from the battle.

The dream can also tell you about your child's personality. If the fortress is formidable, then she could be slightly defensive, insular and wary of things around her. A castle that is cold and uninviting could imply that your child is a little secretive; if it is surrounded by a beautiful landscape and is easily accessible, this indicates that she is romantic and self-contained.

If the interior is in stark contrast to the exterior, then your child is putting on a front for the rest of the world.

Cellars and dungeons

Cellars or dungeons can represent both hidden fears and basic instincts. Dark thoughts may be found here that need to be revealed. Look at what the cellar or dungeon contains: it could be that your child has been naughty recently and has been sent to her bedroom to cool off and contemplate her behaviour.

Dark rooms that are below ground level symbolize repressed impulses. What hidden fears lie in the shadowy depths of a cellar or dungeon? Whatever they are, your child certainly doesn't want to face them at the moment.

There is also a physical link with the stomach and bowels, so could your child be suffering from some digestive trouble?

If the cellar or dungeon is empty, this is a good sign as it means that your child is ready to let in new attitudes and thoughts.

Prisons

A **prison** can be a sign of self-imposed restrictions. Your child could need to let go, but perhaps does not know how. Do you think that she has done something wrong and is feeling guilty, because this prison is entirely of her own making? She could be subconsciously punishing herself for bad things that nobody else knows about or for which she has not been admonished.

Graves and cemeteries

When we find ourselves in our dreams wandering through tombstones in a **graveyard or cemetery**, usually it is to meet a friend or loved one who has died. If this is the case, then your child is seeking reassurance or trying to say something that was left unsaid in real life. She might be wanting to ask forgiveness or simply to tell the person that she loved them.

Everyday buildings

Shops

Shops are representative of choice, and suggest that many options are available – possibly too many. Does your child have a big decision to make? Or, was the shop closed? This would mean the opposite – that your child feels he has no choice in the matter.

What kind of shop was it, and what items were on sale? Does your child need to make up his mind about what he would like for his birthday? Is it a choice between two things that he wants, and he can't decide?

Could it be something more serious, such as choosing whether he lives with his mother or his father? Whatever is the case, perhaps he needs a little extra guidance from an objective adviser.

If your child dreams of sitting in a shop window while passers-by stare and make comment, then he is feeling very uncomfortable or self-conscious about his appearance. Have his milk teeth begun to fall out? Has anybody said anything cruel about the way he looks? On the other hand, if he didn't care that he was being scrutinized, this shows his distrust in people around him and an instinctive belief that people are talking about him behind his back.

Schools

A **school** represents life's lessons from which we must all learn and suggests that we should start listening to the inner teacher within. It is also central to the life of a child, and when a dream involves a school-time issue it is probably wise to interpret it literally, as the chances are that whatever is happening in the dream is reflecting real-life concerns. So, try to build up as clear a picture as possible – there may not necessarily be a problem, just your child subconsciously making sense of something in his life. There may be clues in the dream that will reveal just what it is that he needs to learn at this moment in time.

$$45-8=37$$
$$5\times7=35$$
$$5+4=9$$

Playgrounds and parks

Playgrounds and parks are generally a good sign, as they mean that your child is very happy in all relationships. However, if your child shows any sign of fear, then this could be telling you about some sort of hazard he is facing, particularly if this is a place he goes to regularly. If he is scared of someone hiding in the bushes or behind the trees, then you should keep a careful lookout next time you are there. If your child is allowed to go to the park or playground by himself, ensure that an older, responsible child accompanies him, and emphasize that talking to strangers is not wise. There may be no real cause for concern, but as children frequently blur reality with fantasy, you cannot be too sure.

The path of life

Churches and temples

Churches and temples represent a place of safety and privacy, and are indicators of faith and beliefs. What experience does your child have of religious institutions? Does religion play a big part in her life? In what way would she view entering a church or temple? Is it a place of confession and guilt, or celebration and joy?

A church or temple in a dream is the private place within the dreamer to which she can retreat in order to reflect and make sense of things, and it does not necessarily have to be associated with religion. If your child is entering the building, then it could signify that she is quite often anxious and is seeking the reassurance and comfort of knowing that she is not alone in waking life. Other images that could suggest a similar frame of mind are any place of natural beauty, peace and serenity, such as a deserted beach.

Rivers and roads

A **river** is one of the most common symbols for the journey of life. It can be full of different currents and rapids, twists and bends. Is the river flowing too fast? In that case your child needs to slow down. Is a period on shore required for some rest and reflection?

Water is a symbol of the emotions, so watch out for hints that your child feels as if she is drowning under the demands of others. A **dam** may indicate that someone has created a barrier that has inhibited your child's natural flow.

Hopefully the water is clear and calm, because murky, turbulent water is an indication of clouded judgement and emotional unrest. The best antidote for this frame of mind is a creative outlet through which your child can unleash her feelings. How about a huge canvas and some paints?

A **road** also represents a person's path through life. What hazards and happiness lie along the way? Is there a fork in the road? This means decisions have to be made. If the road is wide then everything is fine, but if it is narrow this means there may be a meeting or encounter that your child has to face. Visits to the dentist, handing in a school project or confessing to that broken window in the greenhouse are all possibilities.

Obstacles across the road, such as walls, can be symbols of difficulties along the way, and if your child is dreaming about being lost along the road, then she may be feeling abandoned and lonely.

Dream interpretation
Objects

Objects

Objects in dreams can be a source of information. What significance do the various elements of a dream have for your child? Are they things to which he has an emotional attachment? Do they play a specific role at certain times in his life? Do they represent a current situation that your child is trying to make sense of and work his way through? You need to make the connection and view these things through the eyes of your child.

Transport

Bikes

A **bicycle** indicates that life can be something of a struggle, as it requires effort on the part of the cyclist to move ahead. But don't worry: your child is making progress, even though it does seem to be very hard work. Where is she going? It would appear that this is one destination she has to reach by herself.

Has your child recently learned to ride a bike, and could this dream be her way of re-living the moment?

If she is riding a **motorbike**, then she is getting frustrated with her present situation and needs to move on. Maybe she needs to be reminded of the old saying, 'patience is a virtue'.

Cars

Cars are the driving force behind a person's journey, so whether your child's dream features a big, shiny red car or a bright yellow taxi, it is important to know whether the dreamer herself drives the car or somebody else is behind the wheel. Who is in control? Are there perhaps moments when your child lets herself be 'steered' by others? Does she actually prefer to let others take all the decisions, or does she fear someone else taking control of her life and leading her into unknown territory? Perhaps, for once, someone should ask her what she would like to do.

If the car is overtaking everybody else, then your child is very ambitious; if the situation is reversed and the car is being overtaken, then she is having trouble accepting that somebody else is better at something than she is. Has her nose been put out of joint lately?

Does being in a car mean anything specific to your child, such as going to school or perhaps on a special journey? What is the most common association your child would have with cars? This

could be simply those in her toy box or, for some poor kids, travel sickness.

Boats

Boats are usually connected with an emotional journey and a period of transition from one stage in life to another. It is important to take note of the type of boat, and how safe and secure it is. Find out what the water is like, as this will show you how your child is feeling. A big boat that is floating on calm waters means all is well on an emotional level, but if you can barely see the boat for all the crashing waves, your child is feeling very vulnerable indeed. Is there an occasion coming up that she is dreading?

Trains

Trains and stations are all about hellos, goodbyes and the need to change. Metaphorically, is your child on the right track? Is he travelling towards the correct destination? Or is it time to change trains? Would you be better off cancelling the piano lessons and buying him a baseball bat? Should you replace football boots with dancing shoes? Maybe your child craves some guidance and support at the moment, and needs to be carried through whatever it is he is experiencing.

Dreaming of running to catch a train or a bus but missing it is a classic anxiety dream, signifying that the dreamer has taken on something for which they feel they aren't quite ready or prepared. Could this be a school performance, or some sort of test?

If your youngster is at the station, it could be that he is waiting for an arrival or for something to happen, or to say goodbye to something he no longer needs. Maybe he feels old enough to take some responsibility now, making his own breakfast or cycling to school without you. Your child needs to move on.

Planes

Planes are concerned with ambitions and plans. Is everything going smoothly, or is it about to come crashing down to earth? Are your child's expectations a little too high at the moment? Conversely, is he expecting disappointment? Has a treat been cancelled one too many times, or do plans keep being changed?

Could it be that your child is worried about somebody 'taking off' and leaving him behind? Or are you taking your child on a plane for the first time, and he is getting nervous?

Dreams of flying high in the sky can indicate that your child is trying to escape the more terrestrial things in life, such as problems or chores. He wants to 'take flight' and flee all his obligations. He may desire a new perspective on life – perhaps he feels bogged down by the opinions of others and wants to formulate his own thoughts and observations.

Using the analogy that flying is leaving Mother Earth behind, then your child could be wanting to break free from a dominating female figure, who may have been over-protective lately.

Aeroplane dreams can also reflect the sensation of out-of-body experiences during sleep.

Obstacles

Bridges

A **bridge** means that choices have to be made, as it is a link between two stages in life.

Is the bridge strong or rickety? This will indicate whether the crossing will be easy or fraught with difficulty. Perhaps certain real-life issues will have to be sorted out before your child can make the crossing to the other side, where there may be a new beginning. Is she about to change schools or go up a grade?

Walls

Walls represent major obstacles that have to be overcome. How does your child deal with the wall? Is it blocking her path? Is it too tall? Does she climb over or go around? Or not even try? Tell her she should fly over it next time.

Fences

Fences are a sign of self-imposed inhibitions and frustrations. Is there something about your child's character that could be impeding her participation in events? Could it be shyness? Or is it possible that you have passed on certain attitudes and beliefs that are restricting your child's behaviour to such an extent that she feels she can't join in with the other kids and let herself go?

Gates

Gates are all about relationships with others. If the gate is large and ornate, then someone is putting up resistance. Could that potential new friend be difficult to play with? If the gate is small and unimpressive, then your child is taking advantage of someone who is being far too compliant.

If the gate is broken and swinging on its hinges, then your child feels that a relationship with someone has been damaged and needs repairing. A rusty gate means that the other person is stubborn and won't accept that changes are necessary. So if there is a rusty gate swinging on its hinges, your child wants to make good but the other person won't budge. Has your youngster been coming home with tales of woe about playground disagreements and fights with her friends?

Doors

Doors symbolize new opportunities and chances, and your child's openness to the outside world and the influence of others. If the dream features a huge, stiff door, then maybe your child considers life to be rather difficult at the moment. A door that is impressive and imposing suggests a level of anxiety about forthcoming events. Does your child have some kind of ordeal coming up, such as public speaking or an appearance in a school play? A locked door indicates a degree of frustration or feeling excluded, whereas an open door means that your child is ready to face whatever comes her way.

Toys, weapons and clothing

Toys

Toys figure so heavily in children's lives that it makes sense that they will turn up in dreams from time to time. They may feature as imaginary playmates who accompany your child on an adventure, or they can have many other meanings. They can represent friends and one-way affection: does your child know someone with whom friendship is not reciprocated?

Dolls usually indicate unhappiness and rivalry. They can represent someone the dreamer dislikes or with whom he has a problem. Could there be jealousy towards a sibling?

Dreaming of a **clown** means that your child is feeling self-conscious and thinks he may have made a bit of an idiot of himself.

Losing a well-loved toy means that your child is feeling very insecure.

Weapons

Weapons are a symbol of defence or attack: your child is either feeling aggressive towards someone or threatened by a person or situation. This is a sure sign that he needs back-up. Whether it's a gun or a silver sword, who is wielding the weapon? Who is being

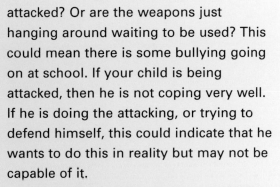

attacked? Or are the weapons just hanging around waiting to be used? This could mean there is some bullying going on at school. If your child is being attacked, then he is not coping very well. If he is doing the attacking, or trying to defend himself, this could indicate that he wants to do this in reality but may not be capable of it.

Remember also to check your child's videos and computer games, as he may simply be playing out a fantasy.

Clothes

Clothes and shoes could mean that your child feels the need to cover up his feelings for some reason. What kind of clothes are they? If they are bizarre or ill-fitting, this usually means that he is not at ease in a particular situation.

The same is true for dreams in which

the dreamer is naked in public, as this means that your child is feeling exposed and vulnerable. Perhaps some secrets have recently come out into the open. Of course, this may not apply if you have a child who hates the restrictions that wearing clothes imposes and sheds them at every opportunity.

If the dream involves shoes there may be a desire to follow in someone's footsteps. Or does your child need to look at life from someone else's perspective and 'walk in their shoes'?

Wearing uncomfortable shoes often means that your child is having a difficult time at the moment due to being unprepared for certain situations. Did you forget to pack his sports kit?

Furniture, containers and keys

Furniture

Furniture has many different connotations for children. It can hold something out of reach, it can be something they are not allowed to climb on, alternatively, it can be a game park where the cushions of the sofa are a cave and the bed is a spaceship. But certain pieces of furniture do have very strong meanings in dreams.

A **mirror** can be interpreted as a reflection of your child's inner self, and usually indicates that she has to come 'face to face' with an aspect of herself that needs to be dealt with. This could be anything from shyness to naughty behaviour. Has she been a little less than honest lately? Have the contents of the cookie jar disappeared rather rapidly?

A **table** is where a dreamer places all their hopes, beliefs and thoughts. What is on your child's table?

An **empty chair** can mean one of two things: a loss or something missing, or an opportunity as the chair is now vacant. What type of chair is it? Does it resemble the favourite chair of someone your child knows, perhaps a departed older relative?

Boxes and cupboards

Boxes and cupboards are all about hidden surprises, secrets and fears.

If your child keeps dreaming of empty boxes or cupboards, then it could mean her life is a little dull at the moment. If she is very nervous about opening the lid or door, then there are deep-seated fears lurking within.

A cupboard that is closed indicates a stubborn attitude. It can also contain skeletons and secrets. What is it that your child is desperate to conceal?

But discovering treasure in one of these hiding places is one of the most positive things your child can dream.

Keys

Keys are symbols of solutions to problems. You will have to consider the context and nature of the rest of the dream to pinpoint what this problem might be. Ask your child what it was she was trying to open, and if she cannot remember or woke up before she found the object that the key was supposed to fit, ask her to close her eyes and imagine what it was.

If the key fits a door, then the solution lies in a change of circumstances. If it is a box or chest, then maybe the answer has been forgotten or suppressed for some reason.

Where was the key found? If it was discovered on a beautiful beach or in a garden, then your child needs some rest and relaxation. If it was in a desk in a classroom, she needs to do some extra studying.

Luggage, food and money

Bags and luggage

Bags and luggage contain life's burdens and emotional baggage. Your child should not have had enough time to gather too much of that, and possibly all these bags represent is a pleasant trip somewhere, or even merely your handbag. But something could be getting to him. What is it that is weighing your child down and hindering his progress?

If the bags are empty, then your child hates to be boxed in or overly committed.

You have a free spirit on your hands.

If your child dreams of unpacking bags and luggage, what is in there? This will be symbolic of things that were packed away at the back of his mind for a while, and now need to be taken out and reassessed. If the contents were of no real importance, then a change of attitude is all that is necessary, as hanging on to the old ways is dragging your child down. Get him to focus on the future not the past.

Food

Food is the symbol of thought – hence the saying 'food for thought'. Too much food in a dream means that there is a lack of focus and unclear intentions towards a person or project. Equally, it could just be the result of your child overdoing it on cake and biscuits at his latest birthday party!

'We are what we eat', so look very carefully at the type of food in the dream. Does your child always dream of sweet or tasty food, or of weird and wonderful dishes that you would never dream of eating? This could tell you about your child's thought patterns.

If he is eating in a dream, this can indicate a need for more contentment or fulfilment. If he is eating with others, then he may need to share his thoughts with you.

Money

Money is associated with protection and security. It can also be linked to health, social status and influence. In a child's eyes, those who have money are powerful: images of kings counting their gold, for example. Quite often, if someone has been ill or very upset they may dream of a surprise windfall of money that somehow makes everything right. This could mean that your child is feeling powerless in a certain situation and wants to be able to reach out and help.

If he keeps dreaming that he has been forced to give all his money away, then there could be a problem with a guilty conscience. What does your child feel he has to 'pay' for?

Dream interpretation
Shapes and Symbols

Shapes and Symbols

Colours, numbers, geometric shapes and other symbols have deep-rooted meanings that can be traced back over hundreds, sometimes thousands of years. We are bombarded daily with images that reinforce our understanding of these symbols, and it doesn't take a child long to absorb this information. But she will also have her own take on these, depending very much on the culture and environment in which she lives.

Shapes

Circles

Circles signify the never-ending cycle of life. They represent the world, the universe and time, and are the symbol of perfection. They can mean that there are many opportunities to come.

A circle is a common symbol of unity. It often indicates the union of conscious and unconscious aspects.

To a child, this shape could be the sun, the moon, the earth, or even a ball, a ring, a plate, an apple, an orange – the list is almost endless.

Squares

Squares mean confidence and security, and can also represent the earth, as they are associated with the quality of being solid.

If you asked your child to think of all things square, he would probably describe building bricks, windows, doors, houses, swimming pools, boxes – the list could go on and on.

Triangles

Triangles are symbolic of the holy trinity – Father, Son and Holy Ghost – and of the three elements of human life – mind, body and spirit.

On a more pragmatic level, in the mind of your child a triangle could be anything from an instrument he plays in the school orchestra to a sandwich or a lump of cheese! Or, it may simply be something he is learning about in his mathematics class.

Hearts

Hearts are seen in much the same way the world over, by adults and children alike, as an emblem of unconditional love. The heart is the organ of the body that generates emotion, the spiritual centre of the body. Is your child taking everything to heart?

Arrows

Arrows indicate direction in life. What are they pointing towards? They can also be poison arrows. Who is being spiteful behind your child's back?

Wheels

Wheels represent fate and fortune. In Buddhism, the eight spokes of the wheel are the paths to enlightenment. The wheel can also be another symbol for the cycles of life. Depending on the circumstances, could it be a warning for your child not to go round and round in circles?

Crosses

Crosses can symbolize the compass; the four elements; health, fertility, life, immortality; heaven and earth; body and soul; the sun and the stars. The cross has religious connotations for Christians, and its interpretation in a dream will depend entirely on what this symbol means to your child.

Colours

Like everything else, colour in a dream is there for a purpose. It can offer healing and guidance, and may be an expression of your child's reaction to the subject matter of the dream.

Some colours, such as white and pink, have very positive connotations, whereas black and grey can indicate negativity. Red, orange, yellow, green, blue, indigo and violet are the colours of the seven energy centres of the body, known as the chakras.

Our understanding of the meaning of colours is deeply rooted in our psyche from a very early age, and different colours will produce instinctive responses and associations in your child.

White

White is the colour from which all others are born. It is symbolic of hope, faith, purity, innocence, perfection, confidence and enlightenment. It is associated with ceremonies of birth, marriage and death. When mixed or associated with other colours, it purifies and refines their meaning. White alone can indicate a proud, rigid, judgemental immaturity – a 'should be', controlling attitude. Soft or pearl white can indicate the gift of prophecy.

Black

Black represents negativity. It is associated with feelings of fear, anxiety, hatred, resentment, guilt, depression and lack of faith. In many cultures and religions, black is also the colour of mourning. Only the Ancient Egyptians saw it as a colour connected with transformation, resurrection and rebirth.

When mixed or associated with other colours, black adulterates and pollutes their meaning, and normally positive colours such as blue take on a more negative interpretation if darkened with black. Seeing things 'in black and white' can also indicates intolerance or a limited way of thinking.

Red

Red is strongly connected to passion and aggression. In healing terms, it can give strength and energy. For the Chinese it is the luckiest colour, but Celtic peoples believed it to symbolize doom and gloom.

The shade of red is important. Scarlet can indicate fun, passion or be a warning of danger. Mix red with black and you get maroon, which indicates frigidity or a sense of foreboding; if you put the two colours together as a combination, this spells anger.

Red and white is commonly associated with blood and tears, which is why it is bad luck to mix red and white roses together. But if they are worn or brought by a healing agent in a dream, it means that they are trying to bring joy and hope.

Orange

Orange is the colour of happiness and healing, particularly to the Japanese and Chinese. Think of the bright robes of the Buddhist monks, which are said to emit a gentle feminine energy that can lift depression and enliven the spirit.

Orange can also be associated with drive, ambition and an independent nature. It is considered to be a hugely energizing colour and, like red, it is used by healers for its stimulating powers. It can also represent the digestive and elimination system. If combined with black, then someone involved is too driven by ambition.

Yellow

Yellow is the colour linked to the intellect and mental powers. Its appearance in a dream may indicate the dreamer's response to the subject matter. It is connected to the ability to rationalize, and if brought by a healing agent it means your child needs help to comprehend certain situations. If, on the other hand, she is wearing this colour in the dream, she fully understands what is going on in her life.

If a guide within a dream brings or wears bright yellow and white, then the dreamer has intuitive or enlightened intellectual powers. If the yellow is next to black, it could mean that something is being thought about too much, and maybe it is time for action.

Green

Green is the colour that represents qualities such as sharing and balance, and it is considered a sacred colour by the Islamic faith. It indicates that the dreamer should be more adaptable and needs to reconcile something within the self, or with another. Very dark green, or green and black, represent difficulties with sharing – this could be jealousy, rivalry or selfishness. Your child may need to achieve better balance in his emotional life by becoming more giving, generous and emotionally open.

Pink

Pink is a mixture of red and white and signifies unconditional love. It has maternal connotations and can mean that your child craves more love and bonding, so you may need to spend a little more time with him. Dark pink or magenta means that he should let go and get on with the flow of life.

Blue

Blue is a sacred colour in many religions around the world. It is associated with spirituality, religion, art, culture, philosophy and the dreamer's attitude to life itself. It is also connected to communication.

If the colour black is mixed with blue, this indicates a negative attitude to life and an inability of your child to express himself. This could reflect superstition or a fearful form of religion. Conversely, light blue is a sign of hope and faith – think how uplifted we feel when we look at a bright blue sky. Quite often in a dream, a healing influence will appear wearing this colour.

Purple

Purple and violet are colours used in many religious ceremonies and rituals (bishops wear purple), and are a sign of a spiritual teacher. They are also associated with higher knowledge and spiritual enlightenment. Anything purple that appears within a dream is a symbol of spiritual learning. The slightly duller version, mauve, is associated with endurance, so maybe the lessons will be tough.

Mixing blue and purple produces indigo, which signifies that the dreamer may have clairvoyant potential, or at the very least be hugely intuitive.

Peach

Peach means empathy and is a signal that your child needs to develop more understanding of other people's situations. It can also indicate that more peace and harmony is needed in his life.

Cream

Cream is the colour of acceptance and indicates that more tolerance is required. It can also mean that your child is growing in maturity.

Grey

Grey is a sign that your child is uncommitted to certain things and there are uncertain or 'grey' areas in his life. It suggests that he is also mentally preventing any outburst of emotion and could be suffering from a degree of depression. There is a lack of colour in his life.

Brown

Brown is associated with practical, earthy matters. It may mean that your child needs to lighten up a little and allow himself to daydream, even to fantasize from time to time. It can also mean that there is a preoccupation with negative material things – maybe he is focusing too much on what other children have and is comparing himself to them.

Silver

Silver is linked with the moon and the deeper side of life, and indicates that your child has the spiritual gift of intuition.

Gold

Gold represents the sun, light and truth in many cultures, and could mean that your child has a spiritual healing gift. It is also a symbol of a growing awareness of new knowledge, which is more valuable than gold itself.

Numbers

Numbers in dreams have the same meaning as in numerology, with each number having its own particular energy and quality.

Always take note of how many objects or people feature in your child's dreams, check the way in which they are grouped and their symbolic significance, and add these meanings to the overall equation. What emerges can sometimes be surprising.

If recording dreams, always include the date. This will allow you to see whether or not your child's dreams have a prophetic quality or any sequential pattern.

0 is associated with the unknowable, unlimited possibility, truth, the source, boundless energy, space, love and God. It symbolizes the fact that we all have infinite potential – but is the dreamer waiting for the right conditions? 'Don't wait' is the clear message here. Your child should take immediate action.

1 represents leadership and ambition, courage, independence, originality, invention and willpower. It is also the symbol of new beginnings and can be suggestive of the first stage of a journey. Or, perhaps your child can sometimes be too aloof and isolated.

2 is the number of balance, of following rather than leading, of harmony, empathy, intuition, diplomacy, partnership, patience and duality. It can also be indicative of a difficult choice, where both options are equally appealing.

3 represents the power of the holy trinity and also the mind, body and spirit, as well as humour, creativity, enthusiasm, the subconscious mind, social skills, communication and imagination. It tells your child to trust her intuition and develop inner strength.

4 is an earthy number that symbolizes the four seasons, elements and points of the compass. It is linked to practicality, order, patience, honesty, stability, loyalty, frugality and responsibility, and is closely concerned with building strong foundations and security.

7 is a highly spiritual number. It represents the universal law of seven and the seven colours of the rainbow and days of the week, as well as deep thinking, wisdom, stoicism, invention, philosophy and all things mystical. A dream focusing on this number may be all about achieving balance of mind, body and spirit, and being fully prepared to do the best your child can.

8 is a practical number, associated with organizational skills, self-discipline, power, success and authority. It is the symbol of achievement. Through the process of rebalancing in life, we often find hidden courage within ourselves. In Buddhism, the lotus is a symbol of spiritual unfolding, and it is usually depicted with eight petals.

5 is the number of the senses, representing freedom, adventure, exploration, love of travel, curiosity, optimism and the need for variety. Think of the five senses, and how if we seek to explore all of them we will become fully realized or whole human beings.

6 has strong family connotations and is associated with nurturing, love, marriage, responsibility, understanding, harmony and perfection within relationships. It is important for each individual to become whole and balanced in order both to give and to receive love.

22 signifies perfection and total completion. It is linked to genius, bridge building, idealism, vision, universal transformation, inspired creativity, alchemy, government and trouble shooting.

33 is the symbol of a Christ-like teacher and healer, which brings with it compassion, protection, blessings, inspiration, honesty and guidance.

9 is associated with humanitarian issues and philanthropy; it also indicates compassion, romance, creativity, wisdom and idealism. We need to appreciate that life has a cycle and a pattern, which in human beings is started by the nine months of pregnancy.

11 is a number of insight and intuition, creativity and angelic channelling. A magical link to visionary and spiritual matters, it brings deep joy and love. It shows a perfect balance and interdependent relationship that must be maintained.

Acknowledgements

Executive Editor **Jane McIntosh**
Editor **Camilla James**
Senior Designer **Rozelle Bentheim**
Design and Artwork **Line and Line**
Senior Production Controller **Louise Hall**

RELIURE
TRAVACTION

A   DEC. 2004